THE TEMPLE OF ETERNITY

KENNIKAT PRESS

NATIONAL UNIVERSITY PUBLICATIONS

SERIES ON LITERARY CRITICISM

General Editor

EUGENE GOODHEART

Professor of Literature, Massachusetts Institute of Technology

RICHARD DOUGLAS JORDAN

THE
TEMPLE
OF
ETERNITY

THOMAS TRAHERNE'S
PHILOSOPHY OF TIME

1972
National University Publications
KENNIKAT PRESS
Port Washington, N.Y. / London

Library of Congress Catalog Card No: 70-189560
ISBN: 0-8046-9019-7

Manufactured in the United States of America

Published by
Kennikat Press, Inc.
Port Washington, N.Y./London

To the memory of my daughter,

Linda Lee Jordan

ACKNOWLEDGMENTS

This study of Traherne's concept of eternity-time and its effect on the *Centuries* is a product not only of my own research but also of the advice, criticism and even the general conversation of many people. I cannot thank all of them individually, but I would particularly like to express my gratitude for the kind and tolerant help of Professor Joseph H. Summers of the University of Rochester. I would also like to thank Professors Lawrence Babb and James Pickering of Michigan State University for reading and commenting on this work, and James M. Osborn of Yale University for allowing me to read and quote from the "Select Meditations" manuscript. Any errors in this study are, of course, my own responsibility.

Contents

THE TEMPLE OF ETERNITY

Thomas Traherne, English clergyman, philosopher, writer and metaphysical poet, was born circa 1636 in Hereford; studied at Oxford in 1656; and became Rector of Credenhill, in Herefordshire, the following year. He died at Teddington in 1674 before attaining the age of forty.

Traherne was scarcely known even to scholars until the discovery of his poems in manuscript, in 1896, in a bookstall. These manuscripts were at first attributed to Henry Vaughan.

Widespread acclaim followed publication of Traherne's *Poetical Works,* edited by Bertram Dobell in 1906, the *Centuries of Meditation,* in 1908, and, in 1910, *Poems of Felicity,* edited by H. I. Bell.

I

"A Philosopher A Christian and a Divine"

The poems and meditations of Thomas Traherne, seventeenth-century Anglican priest, were discovered at the turn of the present century, and critics responded with a wave of enthusiasm. This first wave of acclaim, however, in spite of its apparent magnitude, was rather quick to break and long in being followed by another swell. After the initial celebration of the most obvious qualities of Traherne—a celebration of his striking glorifications of childhood, his bold and enraptured exclamations, his masterful prose,—most critics seemed at a loss what to do with him. Some attempted to make comparisons between Traherne and the Cambridge Platonists but found such comparisons could only be very general. Chapters, articles and dissertations were written dealing with the nature of Traherne's "mysticism." General appreciations, some of them exceedingly perceptive, continued to appear. Yet by the middle or late nineteen forties, after publication of Gladys Wade's speculative *Thomas Traherne: A Critical Biography*, scholarly interest in Traherne was producing little new.

To be sure, some good work on Traherne was done in the fifties; in 1958 H. M. Margoliouth published the first scholarly edition of the *Centuries, Poems, and Thanksgivings*. However, it took until the nineteen sixties for the explosion that had taken place in other areas of literary research to reach Traherne, and it was not until late 1968 that a modern, critical edition of *Christian Ethicks* was finally issued. Some of the new Traherne scholarship has been like that of the past; some of it has gone on to examine Traherne's poetry in terms of the New

3

Criticism; and some has been research into Traherne's ideas, influences and sources. It is to this last category that the present study primarily belongs. In the following chapters I examine an idea and its background, see to what extent Traherne developed this idea, and reach a judgment about the effect this idea had on Traherne's literary productions.

Cited throughout is H. M. Margoliouth's two-volume edition of the *Centuries, Poems, and Thanksgivings,* for the works it contains. The *Centuries* are indicated by *C* followed by the number of the Century in Roman caps and the section in Arabic numerals. The poems and "Thanksgivings" are indicated by title and line numbers. For *Christian Ethicks* the text cited is that edited by Carol L. Marks and George Robert Guffey, abbreviated *CE*; for *Meditations on the Six Days of the Creation,* the reprint introduced by George Robert Guffey. "Select Meditations" is a Traherne manuscript in the Osborn Collection, Yale University Library.

According to the philosophy of Thomas Traherne, time is contained in the ever-present "now" of eternity. Although this idea, in its most elementary form, is not original with him, Traherne carried its implications further than had any previous philosopher. The concept, indeed, is one of the primary footings on which his entire system rests. Therefore, in an effort to gain a better understanding of that system, in the following chapters I have attempted to define Traherne's view of the nature and relationship of time and eternity and to trace the influence of that view in other elements of his thought and art. Traherne's concept and these other elements form a whole; it is difficult and misleading to talk of any one part in isolation. To examine, for instance, what Traherne says of God's eternity without an understanding of how man can have knowledge of such a thing, makes the concept appear more abstract and esoteric than it is and thus, for some perhaps, less reasonable. Yet, since it is impossible to take in the whole in one bite and still be certain of what is being eaten, I have settled on the following divisions for discussion.

I begin with a consideration of what might be called the concept in its absolute or pure state. Neglecting for the present the problem of the limited power of human perception and the road that leads a man up to a vision of the God-nature, I examine Traherne's thoughts about eternity and time. Traherne's own statements, brought together here, establish clearly what he meant by the presence of time in eternity and show that he has made a consistent, systematic formulation. An examination of this formulation in its relationship to past philosophical considerations of the subject and to the views of Traherne's contemporaries not only establishes the place of the concept in the history of thought but also shows the unique extent to which Traherne worked out the details. This historical examination, combined with the original presentation of the concept, counters what seems to be a tendency of some modern readers to regard Traherne's statements about eternity, time and related subjects as hyperbolic metaphors or, worse, solely the results of a childlike perception of a timeless universe.

In the third chapter, having defined the abstract concept of eternity-time (a simplified term meaning the succession of time as it exists in the permanent now of eternity), the next step is to see how human beings can perceive this mode of existence. According to Traherne, man is capable of knowing all eternity even though it is an attribute of the Deity, part of His nature. This chapter is consequently concerned with the infinite capacity of the soul, how the soul by its nature reflects God and thus all of God's attributes. Specifically under study is how the soul in this world not only sees everything in the present moment with its spiritual eye but also, through "Faith" (which is far from being a non-rational acceptance of religious truths), gains sight of the past, and through "Hope" achieves an accurate vision of the future. Traherne bases his method for achieving the ability to see the past and the future on a knowledge of history, for which he takes the Bible as the most reliable text. Thus the study of history in the Bible, combined with application of its examples to the present and future, takes on an immeasurable importance, for it is such activity which unites the soul with eternity, with God. I treat Traherne's view of the soul's capacity, in this third chapter, in its relationship to previous and contemporary philosophies. Since this matter has been discussed by other scholars, my emphasis is on correcting what I believe have been some faulty interpretations of Traherne, rather than on tracing in detail the historical line of thought. Partially of such a nature is the discussion of the soul's perception of space. Other writers have found this an important matter in Traherne, a result of the New Science; yet they neglect

the fact that this perception is inextricably involved in that of
eternity-time. With such an omission, a reader may make the
mistake of taking the limitlessness of space for the infinity of
God in Traherne.

Traherne not only defines eternity-time and the soul which
can know it, he also presents a method by which a sinful,
mortal being may grow into his infinite capacity and gain the
perception of eternity-time, a method that builds on, yet goes
beyond, the study of the Bible as simple history. Traherne says
that man can participate in a three or four-stage process, the
stages of which he names Innocence, Misery-Grace and Glory.
Innocence is the estate of a child when the vision is uncorrupted
as yet by the world. Misery-Grace is that transitional state of
adult life in which a man, having lost his childhood innocence, is progressively released from sin and misery as he works
his way back up to God. Glory is the highest estate of all,
actually realized only after death when the soul finally fulfills all
of its divine nature. This progress takes place not only in
individual human lives but also in the history of the world
itself. Adam, Christ and the New Jerusalem are figures for these
estates in Traherne's works; the stages of human progress
are not only parallel to the spiritual history of the world rep-
resented by these three, but are lived in the fullest through
meditation upon these figures. Traherne's, like Milton's, is a
constantly typological habit of thought, so much so that his
recurrent use of "I" is anything but egotistic, serving as it does
as a device for instruction and a type of "Thou," of Adam, of
Christ and of the soul as it will exist in Glory. The fourth
chapter, then, deals with this progress, this habit of thought and
the things Traherne characteristically associates with each
estate. The progress through these estates is really one leading
the human soul up to all of the divine attributes, but it is
especially a journey to the participation of the soul in eternity.

It is Traherne's *Centuries* that show these ideas about eternity-time and the road to its perception put to their highest
didactic and artistic use. Traherne was not only a religious
teacher and philosopher, but an artist and a skilled craftsman, as
well. He had no noble view of art *per se*, as he shows in
Christian Ethicks where it is defined as

> that Habit, by which we are assisted in composing Tracts and
> Systems, rather then in regulating our Lives, and more fre-

quently appears in Fiddling and Dancing, then in noble
Deeds: were it not useful in Teachers for the Instruction of
others, we should scarce reckon it in the number of Vertues
(p. 24);

still, the art he employed in his instruction of others is surely to
be counted one of Traherne's greatest virtues.

The remaining chapters, then, trace the structure of the *Centuries,* demonstrating the various ways in which Traherne persuades the soul to unite itself with the knowledge of eternity-time. The last chapter touches on some of the "Thanksgivings" as well as treating the Fifth Century because, as explained there, I believe the *Centuries* to be unfinished. Basing an opinion on the opening remarks of the Fifth Century, I feel these "Thanksgivings" may indicate where the remaining sections would have gone. This examination of the *Centuries* provides a picture of the tremendous edifice Traherne has built upon the concept of eternity-time.

It may still seem strange to some readers to talk of Traherne uncompromisingly as a philosopher when past critics have so often treated him as a mystic, an eclectic thinker who "cared little for logic, but gleaned from various theories," or simply a writer of poetic raptures. Even a recent writer is able to describe Traherne as one who "by-passes ratiocination . . . simply by believing implicity in the efficacy of the imagination as an instrument of Knowledge."[1] However, there have always been some who recognized Traherne as a more systematic thinker. Itrat-Husain, for example, though limiting himself by the very nature of his work (*The Mystical Element in the Metaphysical Poets of the Seventeenth Century*), claims: "Thomas Traherne alone of all the mystical poets of the seventeenth century has tried to give us a systematic exposition of his philosophy" (p. 264). Itrat-Husain sees in Traherne a "mind highly trained" (p. 266) with a wide knowledge of Neo-Platonic philosophy. Margaret Bottrall has called Traherne "an extremely consistent and coherent reasoner (if his initial premises be granted),"[2] though she finds his imaginative power more significant. Of great importance in establishing Traherne's relation to philosophy have been the work of Marks and Guffey in their edition of *Christian Ethicks* and the learned articles of Carol Marks (Sicherman) which show the broad background in philosophy Traherne possessed.[3]

At the beginning of the Fourth Century, Traherne, speaking of himself in the third person, tells of his desire to be a philosopher:

> He thought that to be a Philosopher a Christian and a Divine, was to be one of the most Illustrious Creatures in the World; and that no man was a Man in Act, but only in Capacity, that was not one of these; or rather all. for either of these Three include the other two. . . . evry man ought to spend his time, in studying diligently Divine Philosophy. (IV, 3)

It is under the aspect of divine philosophy that this principle of eternity-time comes for Traherne, and its study was one of the major pursuits of his intellectual career. My purpose here is to establish more securely Traherne's position in philosophy, to show how one concept (or set of concepts, if you will), eternity-time, was systematically and consistently developed by him. Admittedly the above outline of this study may not have presented a system that at first glance appears "logical" to the modern mind, unfamiliar with the Scholastic view of eternity. The detailed study of this part of Traherne's philosophy should make it appear somewhat more reasonable, though not necessarily more "true"; for that to be so one would have to accept Traherne's postulates as well as the logic of his conclusions.

Traherne's ideas about eternity and/or time have been discussed before, though briefly, by Robert Ellrodt in *Les Poètes Métaphysiques Anglais* (I, ii, 343-353) and by Elbert N. S. Thompson in his 1929 article, "The Philosophy of Thomas Traherne," in *Philological Quarterly*. In addition, Louis Martz links Augustine's theory of the perception of time with Traherne's in his book *The Paradise Within*; and both Malcom Day and Rufus Jones include a summary of Traherne's concept in their treatments of him, Day in "Traherne and the Doctrine of Preexistence," which appeared in *Studies in Philology* in 1968, and Jones in *Spiritual Reformers in the 16th & 17th Centuries* (p. 335). Other writers as well have made passing remarks about what time was to Traherne, but none have realized the determining power this concept had on so much of Traherne's thinking.

In discussing the structure of the *Centuries*, I enter a field that has had a little more tillage. This subject has been considered by Martz in *The Paradise Within*, by Allan H. Gilbert in "Thomas Traherne as Artist," and by others. Some of these considerations have been simply descriptive analyses of the contents, grouping areas of related subject matter together; one, that of Martz, has attempted to demonstrate the presence of an external pattern, the Augustinian meditation. My own examination is on the whole only slightly related to either of these types, showing a philosophical concept as it determines the structure of an artist's thought, a structure which does not exclude other, simultaneous patterns, but which is more interior, more directly related to specific elements in the thought process of Traherne himself.

My interest in this study is both philosophical and literary, but I must admit that it is predominantly literary. I am not trying to establish Traherne as a member of a school of philosophy, nor am I interested in making a claim for Traherne's original contributions. I am in the main interested in the concept of eternity-time for the value I believe it gives Traherne's art.

Hans Meyerhoff, in his book *Time in Literature*, describes the "literary treatment of time" as an inner, psychological one in which "the causal connections (or associations) between events within memory do not constitute an objective, uniform, consecutive order of 'earlier' and 'later' as they do for events in nature" (p. 22). Meyerhoff labels this quality "dynamic interpenetration," using Bergson's term. It could be debated whether this timeless frame of mind is really characteristic of all great literature. Certainly its importance varies as well as the quality of its use. It reaches perhaps its lowest ebb in the Gothic novel, where the intrusion of the past and future on the present becomes a seemingly supernatural but nonetheless physical one. It reaches its culmination in the novels of Joyce and Proust, in the style of Gertrude Stein,[4] and in the art of Thomas Traherne. Traherne says that man "can se Eternity, & possess infinity" ("Select Meditations," III, 91). When in his writing he participates in this activity, Traherne is not only a Christian divine instructing his fellows in the way of felicity; he is also a literary artist making use of associations which range throughout eternity. Because this use of association is no mere psychological or literary device but an integral part of his philosophy of knowledge, the effect of the concept of eternity-time on his art is all the stronger. Because "mind" for Traherne was a function of the soul, itself the image of God, this "now" of consciousness in his work becomes more nearly universal than for any other writer.

Before beginning an examination of just what the eternal now was to Traherne, I might add a few words about what this work does not do. It does not deal in any detail with matters of Traherne's biography nor recount the history of the discovery of his manuscripts. Nor, with the exception of a lapse in the previous paragraph, does it spend time comparing Traherne with writers and thinkers who followed him by a considerable period. While it may be in some ways interesting to see how Traherne anticipates Blake or Wordsworth, such comparisons do not really do much to explain Traherne. Neither, except in a very general way, do they explain much about Blake and Wordsworth, since neither knew of Traherne. These comparisons do, however, place Traherne in noble company, which is perhaps the intention of those who make them. Yet, to see Traherne as a Romantic is an anachronism that would take a concept of the intermingling of times more confounding than even Traherne's to justify. For similar reasons, no attempt is made here to compare Traherne's view of time with modern views, for example that of Bergson, interesting as such a comparison might be. Though a modern man must of necessity look back with twentieth-century eyes, I try to understand Traherne as he stood in his times and in relation to the history of thought before him. It is hard to look back three hundred years without some distortion of vision, but the attempt should nevertheless be made. For man the past no longer exists when he ceases recalling it.

NOTES

1. Elizabeth Jennings, "The Accessible Art, A Study of Thomas Traherne's Centuries of Meditations," *Twentieth Century*, CLXVII (1960), 143.
2. "Traherne's Praise of the Creation," *Critical Quarterly*, I (1959), 130.
3. Carol Marks Sicherman's articles on Traherne are "Thomas Traherne's Commonplace Book," (1964) ; "Thomas Traherne and Hermes Trismegistus," "Traherne's Church's Year-Book," and "Thomas Traherne and Cambridge Platonism," (1966) ; "Thomas Traherne's Early Studies," (1968) ; and "Traherne's Ficino Notebook," (1969). See bibliography.

4. For a lively discussion of time in the works of a wide range of authors see Madeline B. Stern, "Counter-clockwise: Flux of Time in Literature," *Sewanee Review,* XLIV (1936), 338-365.

II

Eternity-Time

One of the lesser controversies of an age characterized predominantly by religious controversy was over the nature of eternity. The seventeenth century saw a reaction against the Scholastic view that eternity "is entire all at once without any successiveness,"[1] a reaction participated in by such widely different individuals as Thomas Hobbes and George ("Bloody") Mackenzie, persecutor of the Covenanters. This reaction was one, in Hobbes' case at any rate, in favor of what today has become the popular if not necessarily the theological view of eternity, that eternity is an unending length of time, without beginning or end. Hobbes, condemning "vain philosophers," says:

> For the meaning of *Eternity*, they will not have it to be an Endlesse Succession of Time; for then they should not be able to render a reason how Gods Will, and Praeordaining of things to come, should not be before his praescience of the same, as the Efficient Cause before the Effect, or Agent before Action, nor of many other their bold opinions concerning the Incomprehensible Nature of God. But they will teach us that Eternity is the Standing still of the Present Time, a *Nunc-stans* (as the Schools call it;) which neither they, nor any else understand, no more than they would a *Hic-stans* for an Infinite greatness of Place.[2]

And Mackenzie, in his anonymous *Religio Stoici*, also attacks the established doctrine for its unintelligibility: "That Eternity is all present, and that in it, there is neither preterit, nor future, is but a conceit, and a needless mysterie imposed upon our belief, which is really more mysterious then the Trinity" (p. 25).

Thomas Traherne, in spite of his occasional, conventional

12

condemnation of Scholasticism, stood with Aquinas in his philosophy of the nature of eternity, but with an all-important difference: Traherne included time as a part of eternity, a difference which, in his philosophy, reconciles the two opposing camps. Traherne defines eternity in *Christian Ethicks* as "an infinite Length of Duration, altogether present in all its parts in a Stable manner" (p. 67). Even in this simple definition, we see the major adaptation that was necessary in order for Traherne to accommodate eternity to time: the postulation of a permanent *duration* or extension of which the eternal "now" is composed. Again from *Christian Ethicks*: "Eternity is an everlasting Moment, infinite in duration, but permanent in all its parts, all Things past, present, and to come, are at once before him, and eternally together" (p. 184). Thus not only are all things before God in eternity, they are also themselves "eternally together," one period of time being present to another. Perhaps Traherne's view of God's eternity is best summed up in a seemingly paradoxical line of the poem, "The Anticipation": "His Name is NOW, his Nature is forever" (1. 26). The duration of "forever" is in its entirety part of the "now."

For Aquinas eternity was absolutely separate from time. Though God can surely perceive time and all things in it, time itself is not part of His nature; time is mutable. "Eternity is the measure of permanence; time the measure of change."[3] Traherne, however, felt this distinction to be a faulty one. If God can see all of time at once, there can be no change in the whole he perceives; time therefore is all present, complete, thus identical in its attributes to eternity. Time continues to exist as a duration, and though there are differences between the successive units along the immutable line, the line itself is permanent, unchanging, eternal.

"We cannot tell how to conceive," Traherne says, "what the Learned constantly affirm, that all Eternity is at one Time. All I shall observe in Order to the explaining of this Mystery, is onely this, that tho the World begins and Ends with Time, yet Eternity does immutably include Time" (*CE*, pp. 68-69). To include time in eternity Traherne thus does not need to make time infinite in duration; time is not necessarily characteristic of the whole of eternity. Traherne seems to avoid the old argument about whether time existed before the creation of the world, though there is one point where he does suggest the possibility of time existing in all of eternity. Speaking of the place of the "Ages" of time in eternity, Traherne says, "Whether they are commensurat with it or not, is difficult to determine" (C, V, 7). I believe Robert Ellrodt misinterprets Traherne's meaning when he recounts this hypothesis and says of it that, in spite of the fact Traherne neither adopts nor rejects it:

> Qu'il le veuille ou non, le langage du poète, suivant sa forme d'esprit, l'épouse spontanément: ne ménage-t-il pas à chaque siècle une niche dans l'éternité? Ne distingue-t-il pas dans l'éternité même, indivisible par définition, entre les "durées vides" avant que Dieu n'ait créé le monde et les "durées pleines" depuis la Création?[4]

The question is not whether the ages are contained in eternity, as Traherne says definitely that they are, but whether time exists throughout all of eternity, is "commensurat" with it throughout those periods when the world and its time are not. There is no doubt that for Traherne there are durations before and after the life of the world, but whether these durations have the successive nature of time or are in themselves temporally undifferentiated Traherne does not specifically consider. This is not, I believe, from any fear of committing heresy, but simply from a sense of the limit of present perception.

Traherne does feel it necessary, however, to answer the equally involved question of what, aside from the possibility of time, fills that eternity before the creation. What was God doing that he could not have created the world sooner? In the "Select Meditations" (III, 89), Traherne declines to take the way out of the problem offered by the merry theologian cited in Augustine's *Confessions* (Traherne credits the view to Augustine himself) who answered such inquiries with the claim that God during this stage " ' was preparing hell . . . for pryers into mysteries'."[5] Instead, says Traherne, God spent the time (or rather, the duration) doing his homework, preparing to do the best job possible. Traherne presents the same explanation in *Christian Ethicks*:

> All Things were from all Eternity before his Eyes, and he saw the fittest Moments wherein to produce them: and judged it fit in his Wisdom first to fill Eternity with his deliberations

and Counsels, and then to beautifie Time with the execution
of his Decrees.   (p. 183)

This action is not really "before" time, for all things and all
moments are immediately present during it. It is in a measure,
though, outside of time. Though the necessities of language
tend to make statements like the above somewhat ambiguous,
Traherne never really confuses the two characteristics of order
and simultaneity. Both are equally true and have attributes
pertinent to themselves alone.

As quotations in the foregoing discussion indicate, Traherne
often explains the existence of time in eternity through the use
of analogy with physical things in space. Thus eternity is an
object which can be filled and time can occupy a place, as in this
quotation about God's operations in time:

> Among other Objects of Felicity to be enjoyed, *the Ways of
> GOD* in all Ages are not the least considerable and Illustrious.
> Eternity is as much Beautified with them, as his Omnipres-
> ence is with the Works of the Creation. For Time is in
> Eternity, as the World is in Immensity.   (*CE,* p. 111).

And speaking of the fleeting units which are ordinarily thought
to constitute time Traherne says:

> Eternity is a Mysterious Absence of Times and Ages: an
> Endless Length of Ages always present, and for ever Perfect.
> . . . All Ages being but successions correspondent to those
> Parts of that Eternitie wherin they abide; and filling no
> more of it, then Ages can do.   (*C,* V, 7)

Perhaps the most vivid spatial image is in the "Select Meditations" and is concerned with an experience we have all had,
though for us it has been more likely out the window of a car or
train:

> Tis we are Successiv Eternity is not so. Trees in a walk are
> past by, They them Selves Stand Still. And to him that runs
> Seem to run Backward. The moments Stand, we mov by, &
> cry that The Time passeth away.   (I, 95)[6]

Robert Ellrodt has pointed out that *"Même en ses impres-*

sions d'enfance, Traherne n'a jamais séparé le sentiment de l'éternité du sens de l'infini." (I, ii, 346), referring the reader to *Century* III, 3 ("The Corn was Orient and Immortal Wheat, [etc.]"). But it is possible to carry these analogies with space and things in space too far. It must not be assumed that Traherne was really claiming a physical, spatial "place" where all things in time exist. Space and time are two different continua (or extensions, to use the seventeenth-century term) each useful for the illustration of the other because each is contained within an attribute of God. Space is part of God's omnipresence; time, of God's Eternity. The reader will find space discussed in greater detail at the end of the following chapter. The "place" in which all parts of time are present is, however, identical with that in which all parts of space are contained, in that both, though themselves separate, abide in God.[7] *"On comprend alors que le poète nous invite à 'contempler' l'éternité comme un 'object,' "* says Ellrodt (I, ii, 346-347); and he is right. But it must be remembered that the comparison is that of simile; it is not an identification.

To make our own analogy, eternity could perhaps be described as a phonograph record (though it would have to be one of infinite length) along which there runs a needle, you and I in our present moment. The whole record always exists in all its parts; the whole song is on it, but the groove is a line of infinite successive duration of which only one part is at the point of the needle (infinitely small) where the future becomes the past. Even this analogy is only partially successful; for it is the needle that must move, the record stands still, and the movement of the needle is also itself somehow recorded. The needle, in addition, has the power to determine for itself what it will play, though the groove has been cut from eternity by the manufacturer. Thus physical analogy breaks down.

Having defined eternity and the relationship it has to time, we must still determine just exactly what "time" is for Traherne. We have seen something of its nature already; it is a successive duration. That is, although all parts of it may always be in existence, these parts follow a certain established order. The successive units are variously divided up as ages, moments, etc.; but of what, we still ask, do these consist? Of what is time made up? According to Traherne, it consists of nearly everything which is not physical or spatial. Time is filled with acts,

operations, events, all of which have no primary material existence. What holds true for time is, of course, also true for
eternity:

> All the parts of Eternity are filled with Operations, which,
> tho they are one in GOD, like that of shining in the Sun, are
> manifold in Effects, as the Beams of the Sun in their different
> Works among all the Creatures.   (*CE*, p. 69)

This eternality of operations gives tremendous importance to
even the most insignificant human action: "Every little Act we
perform is a fruit & Off-spring of the whole Creation. . . . For
being done it is admitted into Eternity, and shall remain in its
Place, and be visible forever" (*CE*, p. 77).

All acts are not always being enacted by the creatures who
performed them, for that would violate the principle of succession and would also include physical agents in the make-up of
non-physical eternity. "All Acts are Immortal in their places,
being *enbalmed* as it were by Eternity, till the Soul revive and
be united to them" (*CE*, p. 165). (Recall our phonograph
record.) This makes the commission of a sin worse than the
total destruction of the world: "For the World might be
Created again with ease, and all that is in it be repaired with a
word: but a Sin once committed, can never be undone; it will
appear in its place throughout all Eternity" (*CE*, p. 186). In the
"Select Meditations" Traherne tells how all of our tears are
in eternity at the moment when they fell, always present, with
the rest of eternity, to God and to the understanding (I, 93).
But these tears are, of course, symbolic; for "things," the material elements of which creation is made, do not, simply as matter,
live in eternity:

> Wheras things in them selvs began, and quickly end. Before
> they came, were never in Being; do service but for new
> Moments; and after they are gone, Pass away and leav us for
> ever. Eternity retains the Moments of their Beginning and
> Ending within it self.   (*C*, V, 8)

It is this nature of matter that enables Traherne to praise the
human body so highly in some contents and condemn it so
strongly in others; for in its actions it participates in eternity

and can produce something divine. But in its physical existence it is "a Dull Lump of Heavy Clay, by which thou art retarded, rather then doest move" (C, II, 51). There is no indication in this that, as some readers have assumed, Traherne did not believe in the existence of matter. Matter is real; it simply is not made up of the elements characteristic of eternity. It can be affected by the eternal; but without participation in act, matter is dead. Life is operation and is lived in eternity.

The eternal nature of acts does not exclude free will from Traherne's philosophy. Freedom of the will is a primary tenet of his philosophy and intimately related, as it was for Boethius, to the concept of eternity-time. In the succession of time every man has freedom to choose. In eternity the choice may already have been made, but this does not affect the original freedom. Problems about the possibility of free will can arise only when eternity-time's character of succession is confused with its equally real but fundamentally different character of permanence. The question of "will" has nothing to do with this latter characteristic; choices take place only in the succession of time. It is as if we were characters in a movie, not the actors, but the human figures on the screen when the picture is being shown. We do not know the end of the film. We act as we think best in each situation. But the film is in reality complete; and each frame, not just the one in which we appear at the moment, exists without motion in itself, permanent.

Thus there is an eternal "now" which is the simultaneous presence of all parts of time and eternity. This "now" is an infinite, successive duration or extension which we divide into units with our terms "moment," "age," etc.; but which is really one whole, unending continuum, all of which is always in existence. Whether those parts of eternity outside the world's time are also successive Traherne does not decide. The duration of eternity-time holds all acts and operations that have ever been made or ever will be made, though free will is not thereby excluded. Being in eternity, time is contained in an attribute of God.

Ellrodt, then, is misleading when he says that Traherne "conçoit l'éternel non point comme un mode d'existence—l'être même—mais comme un mode de connaissance ou un objet de connaissance" (I, ii, 348). For Traherne eternity is both. One, for that matter, could not exist without the other. Eternity is an object of the understanding because it is being itself and a mode of being. And the answer to Ellrodt's rhetorical question, *"Ne faut-il point conclure que Traherne n'eut point l'intuition véritable de l'éternité, mais seulement de l'éviternité?"* (*ibid.*) is that in reality Traherne reconciles the seemingly irreconcilable notions of eternity and everlastingness; and he does so not by making the two merely different points of view, but by making all the infinite duration of the one the very being, permanent in all its parts, of the other. The contents of eternity are not physical, but this does not make them solely mental. They are spiritual; and though for Traherne mind too is spiritual, it is not for him, as it has become for us, the only spirit. Both spatial and temporal objects can exist in the understanding, but both are still equally "real" and possess individual being. God's eternity has an existence independent of man's comprehension of it.

In two of the above quotations from Traherne he refers to the nature of eternity as a "Mystery" and "Mysterious." Before going any further, it might be well to establish just what "mystery" means in these contexts, since I am trying to present Traherne as a systematic philosopher, and the word may tend to relate the concept of eternity-time to some sort of "mystic" intuition. When Traherne uses the word, it is usually in regard to something for which he proceeds to give an immediate explanation, as in these quotations. Mysteries are not incomprehensible workings of the Deity but rather are hidden truths which can eventually be understood. Traherne states the purpose of his explaining of mysteries in the prefatory poem, "The Author to the Critical Peruser":

The naked Truth in many faces shewn,
Whose inward Beauties very few hav known,
A Simple Light, transparent Words, a Strain
That lowly creeps, yet maketh Mountains plain,
Brings down the highest Mysteries to sense
And keeps them there; that is Our Excellence:
At that we aim; to th' end thy Soul might see
With open Eyes they Great *Felicity*,
Its Objects view, and trace the glorious Way
Whereby thou may'st thy Highest Bliss enjoy.
(11. 1-10)[8]

In his emphasis on the rational explanation of mysteries, ✓

Traherne is like the Cambridge Platonists, particularly Henry
More. In his *Divine Dialogues,* More seems to be making fun of
those who would make something recondite out of philosophy when he has Cuphophron defend himself with the exasper-
ating claim, *"Metaphysicks* were not *Metaphysicks, Hylobares,*
if they were not mysterious" (I, 150). More gives his own
definition of "mystery" at the opening of his book, *An Explanation of the Grand Mystery of Godliness,* a definition that accords
with Traherne's use of the word:

> Every legitimate *Mystery* comprehends in it at least these
> Four *Properties. It is a piece of Knowledge,* First, *competent-
> ly Obscure, Recondite and Abstruce:* That is, It is not so
> utterly hid and intricate, but that, in the Second place, *It is in
> a due measure Intelligible.* Thirdly, *It is not only Intelli-
> gible, what is meant by it;* but it is *evidently and certainly
> True.* Fourthly and lastly, *It is no impertinent or idle Specu-
> lation,* but a *Truth very Usefull* and *Profitable:* We may well
> add also, *for some Religious End.*   (p. 1)

Traherne's explanation of the mystery of eternity-time was
built on premises not necessarily original to him, though the
elaborate structure he built on these premises is unique. The
elements of Traherne's basic concept had both ancient and
contemporary parallels.

Aquinas' belief in the eternal "now," divorced from time, has
already been mentioned. The origin, however, of the doctrine
that there is an unchanging, stable eternity is traditionally attributed to the philosopher Parmenides. Though a recent com-
mentator and translator of his poem has denied the validity of
this, maintaining that in reality "Plato was the first Greek
philosopher to grasp the notion of atemporal eternity and to
distinguish it from the perpetuity of infinite duration."[9] In the
seventeenth century, Ralph Cudworth, another of the Cambridge Platonists, expresses what has been the usual view of this
pre-Socratic philosopher. In his monumental though incomplete
True Intellectual System of the Universe, Cudworth credits
Parmenides with believing in a supreme Being who was

> altogether immutable or unchangeable, whose duration there-
> fore was very different from that of ours, and not in a way of
> flux or temporary succession, but a constant eternity, without

either past or future. From whence it may be observed, that this opinion of a standing eternity, different from that flowing succession of time, is not so novel a thing as some would persuade, nor was first excogitated by Christian writers, schoolmen or fathers, it being at least as old as Parmenides. (II, 42-43)

Traherne was familiar with Plato's dialogue, the *Parmenides*, or at least with Ficino's epitome, since he copied about half of Ficino's *"argumentum"* to it (glossing over a portion with a summarizing phrase) in the "Ficino Notebook."[10] The *argumentum* summarizes the various hypotheses of the dialogue *"vel de uno rerum omnium principio, vel de Idaeis"* without any specific application to eternity or time. But, of course, in the dialogue itself Traherne would have found the hypothesis that the One "cannot be older or younger, or of the same age, either with itself or with another. . . . cannot be in time at all."[11]

For Plato, whether or not it was true for Parmenides, there was a timeless, unmoving eternity. Though time was created a moving image of that eternity, as he says in the *Timaeus,* it nonetheless remained absolutely separate from it. This separation of time and eternity was reinforced by Plotinus who in the *Enneads* stressed that "Eternity and Time" were "two entirely separate things."[12] Plotinus defined eternity as:

a Life changelessly motionless and ever holding the Universal content (time, space and phenomena) in actual presence; not this now and not that other, but always all; not existing now in one mode and now in another, but a consummation without part or interval. All its contents is in immediate concentration as at one point; nothing in it ever knows development: all remains identical within itself, knowing nothing of change, for ever in a Now, since nothing of it has passed away or will come into being, but what is now, that is ever. (III, vii, 3, p. 224)

Though the material of time is present to eternity like a mirror image to its beholder, time as it actually exists does not have an eternal nature. Rather than being only an image, as it was for Plato, time for Plotinus was "a descent from Eternity" (III, vii, 7, p. 229), the result of a progressive downward development from the eternal.[13]

It is to the medieval Christian philosophers we must turn to
find the precedent for Traherne's explicit inclusion of time in
the "now" of eternity, going first to Boethius. Marks and Guffey,
in their edition of *Christian Ethicks*, note that Traherne's definition of eternity as "an infinite Length of Duration, altogether
present in all its parts in a Stable manner" (p. 67)

> appears close to that of Boethius in *De consolatione philoso-
> phia*, V. 6 (Chaucer's translation): "Eternite . . . is parfit
> possessioun and altogidre of lif interminable." (p. 330n.)

These parallel passages do point out an important relationship
between Traherne and Boethius. Not that, in both, eternity is a
permanent "now"; for, as we have seen, this antedates Boethius.
But that, in both, eternity is in some measure a *duration* ("lif
interminable") as well. However, the really significant similarity of these two philosophers is only implied in the quoted
passages: for both *time*, past, present and future, is a part of
durational eternity. Boethius, after the passage quoted by Marks
and Guffey, goes on to talk of the mutability of things in
time; and Traherne also acknowledges that, to human perception, time passes. But human perception is not necessarily God's,
is not absolute; and Boethius concludes his remarks on this
subject by saying that God,

> comprehending this infinite space of that which is past and to
> come, confideth al things in his simple knowledge, as though
> they were now in doing. So that, if thou wilt weigh his
> foreknowledge, with which he discerneth all things, thou wilt
> more rightly esteeme it to bee the knowledge of a never
> fading instant than a foreknowledge as of a thing to come.[14]

That this "knowledge" of God's is an actual participation, not
simply a proximity as it was for Plotinus, Boethius makes clear
in his tractate, "De Trinitate":

> But the expression "God is ever" denotes a single Present,
> summing up His continual presence in all the past, in all the
> present—however that term be used—and in all the future.
> Philosophers say that "ever" may be applied to the life of the
> heavens and other immortal bodies. But as applied to God it
> has a different meaning. He is ever, because "ever" is with

Him a term of present time, and there is this great difference between "now," which is our present, and the divine present. Our present connotes changing time and sempiternity; God's present, abiding, unmoved, and immoveable, connotes eternity.[15]

Boethius' view of the participation of time in eternity is echoed and developed by St. Anselm, whom Traherne mentions in the *Centuries* (I, 91). Anselm discusses the matter both in the "Proslogion" and the "Monologion," and it is not unlikely that Traherne would have been familiar with these.[16] In the "Monologion," Anselm defines the eternity of God somewhat as Boethius did, "an interminable life, existing at once as a perfect whole."[17] He clears up a point that in Boethius could tend toward ambiguity, saying of eternity:

If the usage of language permitted, it would, therefore, seem to be more fittingly said that it exists *with* place or time, than that it exists *in* place or time. For the statement that a thing exists *in* another implies that it is *contained* more than does the statement that it exists *with* another.   (p. 81)

Thus though, according to Anselm, God is "simultaneously present in every place or time" (p. 80), space and time do not limit his existence. For Anselm and Traherne space and time are merely elements of infinity and eternity. "For just as an age made up of times contains all temporal things, so thy eternity contains the ages of time themselves."[18]

Anselm's view, however, was not that which prevailed in Christian thought. Aquinas' rejection of the inclusion of time in eternity came about even though he used Boethius as the authority for his definition of eternity. But even before Boethius saw the two united in God, St. Augustine had made the contrast between time and eternity which became characteristic of the main stream of Christian thought. In his *Confessions*, Augustine asks of eternity:

Who shall hold it, and fix it, that it be settled awhile, and awhile catch the glory of that ever-fixed Eternity, and compare it with the times which are never fixed, and see that it cannot be compared; and that a long time cannot become long, but out of many motions passing by, which cannot be prolonged altogether; but that in the Eternal nothing passeth, but the whole is present; whereas no time is all at once present.[19]

This insistence on the contrasting nature of eternity and time, a separation so absolute that, as Gregory of Nyssa put it, "extensions in time find no admittance in the Eternal life,"[20] is fundamentally different from the Platonic doctrine in which the separation that exists is one of an object and its mirror image, the emphasis there being on the similarities in spite of the separation; and it is absolutely different from the doctrine of Boethius, Anselm and Traherne. The reluctance of Christian thinkers to enshrine the mutations of time in eternity is, of course, understandable. Such an incorporation would seem to violate the basic dichotomies of a religion which postulates compensation in another world for the evil in this and which asks its adherents to renounce the world, the flesh and the Devil. It is not necessarily a different religion, but certainly a very different emphasis which enables men like Traherne to see opposites contained in each other, the world an object for love and thanksgiving, the flesh able to express the divine attributes, and evil working in spite of itself to produce good. Such an emphasis results from a sight acutely aware of the oneness of being. Traherne's method of thought is that of the reconciliation of opposites; his greatest reconciliation, that of time and eternity.

In Traherne's own period there was, as already noted at the beginning of the chapter, a reaction against the traditional notion of eternity as a permanent "now." The alternative idea, an "Endlesse Succession of Time," revived by Hobbes, had always been opposed on the basis of Aristotle's stipulation that it was impossible to have a series without a first term. Ralph Cudworth makes an attack on the idea of an "everlasting" eternity from this direction, showing that a belief in the eternal extension of past time would result in "an infinity of time past which was never present" (II, 528)—a logical impossibility. He nevertheless claims the necessity of something being of infinite duration; but, in spite of "Atheists" who will "smile, or make faces, and show their little wit in quibbling upon nunc-stans, or a 'standing now' of eternity" (II, 529), he says this infinite duration can be characteristic only of God, and, unlike time, it is a "permanent duration, never losing any thing of itself once present, as sliding away from it, nor yet running forwards to meet something of itself before, which is not yet in being" (II, 529). Thus, like Traherne, Cudworth incorporates duration into his concept of eternity; unlike Traherne, he excludes the duration of human time. For Cudworth, the words "infinite and eternal" are "attributes belonging to the Deity, and to that alone" (II, 532). Man apparently can conceive of this eternity, but he does not experience it.

While Traherne and Cudworth tried in their own ways to reconcile the notion of infinite duration with that of the permanent now, others reacted differently. John Bramhall condemns the whole of Hobbes' view in *The Catching of Leviathan*, claiming that its result is to make God into something finite. "Our God," he says, "is immutable without any shadow of turning by change, to whom all things are present, nothing past nothing to come. But *T.H.* his god is measured by time, loosing something that is past, and acquiring something that doth come every minute."[21] Not quite so uncompromising is John Bartlet (whose use of "estates" parallels Traherne's).[22] Bartlet solved the problem by favoring both sides simultaneously:

> There is a double Eternity; one *a parte ante*, and another *a parte post*; one that hath neither beginning nor end, another that hath a beginning, but no end. For the first; so God onely is Eternal. . . . For the other Eternity . . . This is the Eternity of Angels and Men.   (*The Practical Christian*, p. 241)

Thus for Bartlet eternity and sempiternity are equally real, but different modes of being.

Marks and Guffey, in a note to *Christian Ethicks* (p. 331), point out that Traherne had read two contemporary works containing discussions of eternity: Henry More's *Divine Dialogues*, vol. I (London, 1668) and Thomas Jackson's *Treatise of the Divine Essence and Attributes* (London, 1628). Both of these works propose an eternity which is, like Traherne's, a permanent "now" containing all the succession of time. Neither develops the idea beyond the brief remarks quoted by Marks and Guffey. Traherne's editors, however, misread the lines they cite from Henry More when, after quoting Hylobares' definition of eternity, "That it is an essential presence of all things

with God, as well of things past, present, as to come; and that
the Duration of God is all of it, as it were, *in one steddy and
permanent . . . Instant at once,*" they go on to say, "Philotheus
stigmatizes this description as a 'Notion of Eternity that some
have rashly pitched upon'." What is being stigmatized is *not* this
definition but the implication which Hylobares draws from
it and finds a contradiction: that past, present and future are in
eternity and yet "that eternall Duration should be indistant to
itself, or without continuation of Intervalls" (More, p. 59) or,
in other words, that eternity contains a succession, time, but yet
is not in itself successive. The view More is reacting to is not a
fabricated one but is expressed by at least one other contemporary of Traherne, Robert South. In regard to eternity, South
says that it "nonplusses the strongest and clearest conception, to
comprehend how one single act of duration should measure all
periods and portions of time, without any of the distinguishing
parts of succession."[23] South is content, however, to let the
mystery stand.

It is to this contradiction rather than in opposition to the
original definition that Philotheus offers the solution quoted by
Marks and Guffey:

> That the whole Evolution of Times and Ages from everlast-
> ing to everlasting is so collectedly and presentifickly rep-
> resented to God at once, as if all things and Actions which
> ever were, are, or shall be, were at this very Instant, and so
> always, really present and existent before him.   (quoted
> *CE*, p. 331n.)

Philotheus does not in the least amend the first definition but
removes the suggested contradiction by showing the continued
existence of succession in the duration of God's now.

> Continuity of Duration is also competible to the Divine Exis-
> tence, as well as *Eternity* or *Life eternall* . . . The Compre-
> hension of the Evolution of all Times, Things, and Transac-
> tions is permanently exhibited to God in every moment of
> the succession of Ages.   (More, pp. 60-61)

Thus there is no confusion of separate times nor a chaotic
mixing together of all things temporal. Everything exists, as
Traherne would phrase it, in its place. Eternity, then, is defined

conventionally enough by More. In his philosophical poem, *Psychozoia*, he says:

> Joyfull *Eternity*
> Admits no change or mutability,
> No shade of change, no imminution,
> No nor increase; for what increase, can be
> To that that's all?   (p. 3)

But eternity for him also includes infinite, permanent duration and the limited succession of time. For More as for Boethius, Anselm and Cudworth, however, this eternity of God is still apart from the world as men perceive it. "The Duration of *God* is like that of a *Rock*, but the Duration of *natural things* like that of a *River*" (*Divine Dialogues*, I, 64). Time as it exists in eternity becomes something like what Newton would describe as absolute time, real but basically unknowable in its true nature. It is in making eternity-time applicable to human experience and available to human knowledge that Traherne parts company with his predecessors and contemporaries in the concept.

To what Marks and Guffey give from Thomas Jackson, I would add that Jackson, like Traherne, explains eternity through its analogy to infinity or omnipresence. "Whatsoever hath beene, or rightly may be conceived of divine immensity," says Jackson, "will in proportion as well suit unto eternity" (p. 62). And when Traherne says that "Time is in Eternity, as the World is in Immensity" (*CE*, p. 111), he echoes Jackson's remark that "There is no period of time to us imaginable, which is not so invironed by Eternity, as the Earth or Center is with the Heavens; save onely that the Heavens are finite, and Eternity infinite" (p. 78). In addition to the views of the authors listed by Traherne's editors, Jackson also cites Boethius' idea of eternity. Thus, whether Traherne read Boethius or not, he would have been familiar with his definition. It is Boethius' view that Jackson adopts as his own.

Before leaving Traherne's seventeenth-century English contemporaries, I should take note of a statement by Joan Webber in her book, *The Eloquent "I."* She remarks there that for all the conservative Anglicans, as she calls the group of writers in which she includes Traherne, "time . . . is an aspect of eternity; there is nothing new under the sun; every

man is like Adam, who contained all" (p. 7). Miss Webber
qualifies this in a note by saying, "I am considering this literary,
ideological view of time as literary characteristic, and do not
intend to suggest that in his writing or out of it the Anglican is unaware that chronological time governs the daily lives of
men" (p. 269). Though Traherne was certainly aware of
chronological time, he alone of all the major "Anglican" literary
figures of the seventeenth century actually claimed time's
existence under the aspect of eternity as part of his philosophy
of being. For even Vaughan, who "saw Eternity the other
night," in its old Neo-Platonic circle, saw it completely separated from Time "In which the world / And all her train were
hurl'd."[24]

Elbert N. S. Thompson compares Traherne with another
contemporary thinker who certainly did see time *sub quadam
aeterni specie*, Benedict de Spinoza. A large part of the trouble
in comparing Traherne to Spinoza (the same trouble critics
have had in comparing Traherne to Berkeley) is not so much in
determining Traherne's position as in determining that of
the second half of the comparison. On the matter of eternity
and its relationship to time, Spinoza was anything but clear.
Modern scholars tend to agree, however, on what Spinoza
meant.

Thompson says that "by eternity [Spinoza] means not an
unending period of time, but the infinite completeness of God
. . . Eternity denotes not a continuance of existence, but a manner or quality of existence" ("Philosophy of Traherne," pp. 104-
105). Thompson cites H. H. Joachim's *Study of the Ethics
of Spinoza* to support his view that this manner of existence
is, according to Spinoza, one in which the human mind can
participate, viewing things in time under the aspect of eternity. Rosalie Colie, in a note to her 1957 article, "Thomas Traherne and the Infinite: The Ethical Compromise," published in the *Huntington Library Quarterly*, calls "Thompson's
statement on Traherne's likeness to Spinoza's view . . . wrong,
the result of the deceptive similarity in the vocabulary of ideas
that tends to obscure seventeenth-century distinctions to us." It
is difficult to see how Thompson's comparison is "wrong," except in being too limited. There are points of difference in the
two time-philosophies; yet, in that both view eternity as a state
of being which is "not an unending period of time," and in that

both claim the human mind can see things in time under the aspect of eternity, they are comparable, and these are the comparisons Thompson makes.

It is necessary, however, to point out that though all things exist in eternity, time itself, for Spinoza, is not necessarily a real thing. Spinoza's doctrine, according to H. F. Hallet, "conceives created beings, whether finite or infinite, to be eternal, and durational beings fragmentary and confused privations of such eternal beings as 'projected' or the 'reference system' of the individual."[25] Thus time for Spinoza is the result of corrupted perception and its succession has really nothing to do with the now of eternity, as it does for Traherne. Spinoza, according to Émile Bréhier, has a three-part system by which man progresses from time to eternity; but the progress is simply a change in the method of perception until things are seen in their eternal nature.[26] The important point for a comparison of Traherne and Spinoza is that in spite of differences in points of view, for both all creation exists *in* eternity. "I understand ETERNITY," says Spinoza, "to be existence itself."[27]

For Traherne and Spinoza eternity was not only a possession of God but was equally available to man. For Traherne, at least, this was due to the nature of the human soul, created in the image of God. It is therefore appropriate to ask next just what the nature and power of the soul was for Traherne and, specifically, how man knows himself to live in God's eternity.

NOTES

1. Thomas Aquinas, *Summa Theologica*, Ia, x, 1, in *St. Thomas Aquineas: Philosophical Texts*, trans. and ed. Thomas Gilby, p. 83.

2. *Leviathan*, pt. 4, chap. 46, ["Everyman" ed.] intro. A. D. Lindsay, p. 370.

3. *Summa*, Ia, x, 4, Gilby, p. 83.

4. *Poètes Métaphysiques*, I, ii, 347.

5. [Modern Library ed.] trans. Edward B. Pusey, p. 252.

6. The same image is used, with a ship and the shore substituted for the runner and the trees, in *C*, V, 8. Images for eternity in the *Centuries* are discussed briefly by Zenos Johan Bicket, "An Imagery Study in Thomas Traherne's Centuries of Meditations" (diss. University of Arkansas, 1966), pp. 100-102.

7. Malcom M. Day recognizes that for Traherne time is contained in eternity, but he wrongly labels this part of "the doctrine that time is the moving image of eternity" ("Doctrine of Pre-existence," *SP*, LXV, 90). Aside from the historical differences of the two positions, discussed below,

this takes for an image what is an identity. This is all the more surprising since the major part of Dr. Day's article takes for an identity what is really an image, the soul and its relationship to God, a problem discussed in Chapter IV.

8. For examples of this use of "mystery" in the *Centuries* see I, 3; I, 100; II, 3; III, 81; and IV, 81.

9. Leonardo Taran, *Parmenides*, p. 187.

10. British Museum MS. Burney 126, f. 17. For a general description of the notebook see Carol Marks Sicherman, "Traherne's Ficino Notebook."

11. *The Dialogues of Plato*, trans. B. Jowett, II, 104.

12. III, vii, 1, trans. Stephen MacKenna, p. 222.

13. Ellrodt contrasts Plotinus to Traherne (I, ii, 348), and Marks and Guffey refer the reader to Plotinus in connection with Traherne's view of eternity (*CE*, p. 330n.).

14. "I.T.'s" translation of the *Consolation of Philosophy*, ed. William Anderson, p. 116.

15. *Boethius, The Theological Tractates*, [Loeb ed.] trans. H. F. Stewart and E. K. Rand, p. 21.

16. Anselm had been in print almost since the introduction of movable type. Seventeenth-century editions of his "complete works" were published by Joannis Picardi (Cologne, 1612), Theophilus Raynaud (Lyons, 1630), and Gabrielis Gerberon (Paris, 1675).

17. *Saint Anselm: Basic Writings*, trans. S. N. Deane, p. 83.

18. Anselm's "Proslogion" in *A Scholastic Miscellany: Anselm to Ockham*, ed. and trans. Eugene R. Fairweather in *The Library of Christian Classics*, ed. John Baille *et al.*, x, 87.

19. P. 251. The question of Augustine's theory of the human perception of time, a very important one in determining his relationship to Traherne, is discussed in the next chapter.

20. *Against Eunomius*, I, 42, in *Nicene and Post-Nicene Fathers*, ed. Philip Schall and Henry Wace, v, 100.

21. In *The Works of . . . John Bramhall*, (Dublin, 1676) p. 873.

22. See *CE*, p. 307n. and Chapter IV of the present study.

23. *Sermons Preached Upon Several Occasions*, I, 10. South has much to say that is like Traherne about the power of the human soul, a matter discussed in the next chapter. South entered Oxford in December 1651, a little less than sixteen months before Traherne matriculated. He was made public orator of the university in 1660.

24. "The World," ll. 1, 6-7, in *The Works of Henry Vaughan*, ed. L. C. Martin, p. 466.

25. *Benedict de Spinoza: The Elements of His Philosophy*, (London, 1957) p. 48.

26. *The History of Philosophy: The Seventeenth Century*, trans. Wade Baskin (Chicago, 1966) pp. 183-185.

27. *Spinoza's Ethics* [Everyman ed.], trans. Andrew Boyle, p. 2. Spinoza was known in England in Traherne's lifetime, and Henry More was acquainted with his work; but the *Ethics*, which contains the primary materials on Spinoza's view of eternity, was not published until after Spinoza's death in 1677.

III

The Temple of Eternity

While Traherne saw time and space as part of God's eternity and immensity, he did not, like the "Familists" whom Theophilus Gale condemns in the *Court of the Gentiles*, believe *all* existing things to be "particles of God."[1] Matter, as we have said, though it has being, does not exist in the eternal; it can, nevertheless, be affected by it. Of a very different nature, though still not part of God, is the soul. The soul is spiritual, the image of God, potentially able to reflect all of God's attributes, thus infinite in its capacity for eternity and immensity.

The idea of the infinite capacity of the soul was a common one in Renaissance Platonism, coming to Traherne's England largely from the writings of Ficino and from Ficino's publishing and publicizing of Hermetic and Platonic documents. Traherne, ever reconciling, interprets the doctrine of the unlimited soul through his concepts of "Faith" and "Hope," thus Christianizing the idea to a greater extent than it had been while making it compatible with his concept of eternity-time. In addition to Faith and Hope, Traherne employed the basic assumptions of Renaissance faculty psychology in developing his philosophy of the infinite capacity of the soul, thus, in the end, demonstrating the ability of the soul to perceive eternity-time on philosophical, religious and psychological grounds. In discussing these grounds, I begin by examining what Traherne has to say of the soul's relationship to the body, go on to treat the soul's likeness to God, examine the historic background of Traherne's basic concept of the soul, and then, having established this groundwork, deal specifically with Traherne's philosophy of the soul's perception of eternity-time.

We saw in the last chapter that the reason why Traherne

31

could condemn the human body so strongly at some times and
yet also write such things as the "Thanksgivings for the Body"
was because a body, being matter, does not partake in the
nature of God but is, in essence, dead. Yet, as it is used to
express *actus*, the bodily form does in a manner participate in
divinity. The primary *actus* which the body expresses is the
soul; and because the soul is the image of God, the body,
however indirectly, expresses Deity. The "Thanksgivings for the
Body" show how this "Dull Lump," once it is given form
(and "form" is not physical) expresses spirit even in its parts.
For God made

> Limbs rarely poised,
>   And made for Heaven:
> Arteries filled
>   With celestial Spirits:
> Veins, wherein Blood floweth,
>   Refreshing all my flesh,
>   Like Rivers.
> Sinews fraught with the mystery
>   Of wonderful Strength,
>   Stability,
>   Feeling.
> O blessed be thy glorious Name!
> That thou hast made it,
>   A Treasury of Wonders,
>   Fit for its several Ages;
>   For Dissections,
>   For Sculptures in Brass,
>   For Draughts in Anatomy,
> For the Contemplation of the Sages.
> Whose inward parts,
> Enshrined in thy Libraries,
>   The Amazement of the Learned,
>   The Admiration of Kings and Queens,
> Are The Joy of Angels;
>   The Organs of my Soul,
>   The Wonder of Cherubims.
>   (48-73)

The body itself is but an organ of the Soul and, as Traherne
says in *Christian Ethicks* (p. 47), useless without it. As the soul
stands in regard to the body, so the body is to the world: "The
visible World was made for the sake of these Bodies, and with-

out such persons as men are, it would be utterly useless" (*CE*, p. 104). Thus the entire value of the physical creation (though not the *being* of it) rests ultimately for Traherne upon the activity of the soul within it. We noted that it is action, operation, which, being spiritual, dwells in eternity-time. Traherne recognized that all actions, like the soul itself, have a physical expression. Yet even this visible manifestation of an action is worthless except for its spiritual, inner, cause and nature. As the body is to the the soul, so are actions as they appear in the world to the divine Act.[2] This is not to say that the soul could not exist without the body; it can and, after death, does. But, in keeping with the principle of plenitude, God made man a combination of body and soul in order that all possible things might have value as well as being.[3] Man, however, must at last leave the things of the body behind, realizing that the value these things have comes from their relation to his soul rather than from anything in their independent existence. Man has come mistakenly to take his bodily existence for his real being, but "you are never your true self, till you live by your Soul more then by your Body" (*C*, II, 92). You must come out from "under the Disguise of this apparent Clod" in order to find yourself "a mighty Great and Coelestial Personage, a Divine and Glorious Creature, Miraculous and Mysterious, even the Image of the Deity" (*CE*, p. 168).

Man's soul is the image of God, but it is not God. Malcom Day, in his article on "Traherne and the Doctrine of Pre-existence," asserts: "Traherne identifies God and the Soul *in essence*."[4] He seems to take Traherne's statements about the infinite capacity of the soul and parallel remarks about the infinite nature of God as referring to one and the same thing. Thus there are not in reality many individual souls, but one World Soul of which individual souls are deprived participants. In response to this, the historical position of Traherne could perhaps be cited, for Traherne lived in a time when it would have been all but impossible for him to believe that all souls are really one. The Averroist heresy had been attacked in earnest by Ficino, but it was really a dead horse when Henry More took a stick to it in *Antimonopsychia, or That all Souls are not one.*[5] However, Traherne himself says clearly that souls are images of God, that they are created, and that they are many.

"For he hath made my Soul / In the Image of himself" ("Thanksgivings for God's Attributes," 9-10). In the *Centuries*

Traherne goes so far as to say that even if God had wanted to
make a soul identical with himself he could not have done so:
"It is no Blasphemy to say that GOD cannot make a GOD: the
Greatest Thing that He can make is His Image" (III, 61). God
has placed in our souls not his actual power but rather, "he
hath implanted the Similitude of his power" (*CE*, p. 52). Man
should love everyone as God does, "for this will make a man the
Image of GOD, and fill him with the mind and spirit of
Christ, it will make every man that is, the Representative of GOD
and of all the World unto him" (*CE*, p. 253). One soul is of
infinite capacity, but "the Existence of many Souls is so far from
abating the value of one, that it is by reason of their multitude more useful and Excellent" (*CE*, p. 38). And, of course,
because of their spiritual natures all souls can possess infinity
and eternity without any conflict of ownership. Thus it would
be a serious error to edit out the plural form of "soul" in
Traherne.

That Traherne believed the soul to be of unlimited capacity,
as Day and many other readers recognize, is beyond question.
Traherne, as Rufus M. Jones says, "is never tired of declaring
the infiniteness of the human soul."[6] In his poetry Traherne
sings of "A vast and Infinit Capacitie" that "did make my
Bosom like the Deitie, / In Whose Mysterious and Celestial
Mind / All Ages and all Worlds together shind" ("Silence,"
75-78). "Free Souls can know no Bound," he says in "The City"
(55). And in *Christian Ethicks* Traherne explains that "the
Sphere of [the soul's] Activity is illimited, its Energy is endless
upon all its Objects. It can exceed the Heavens in its Operations, and run out into infinite spaces" (p. 40). In the "Select
Meditations" Traherne specifies four ways in which the soul's
infinity is like that of God: in its omnipresent extension, in its
immortal duration, in its spiritual essence, and in its value (II,
28). In containing these attributes the soul becomes sanctified,
and Traherne constantly refers to it as a temple:

        . . . a Temple unto God.
    A living Temple of thine Omnipresence.
        An understanding Eye.
    A Temple of Eternity.

    ("Thanksgivings for the Soul," 18-21)

And in this temple may be contained everything that is. "All things are penetrable to the Soul of Man. / All things open and naked to it" (217-218).

This belief in the infinite power of the soul is typical, as I have said, of many thinkers in the Renaissance. But those thinkers merely developed ideas inherent in the ancient philosophers: "There's a greatness," says Seneca, "an aristocracy in the soul of man. It will suffer the setting of no limit but such as it shares with God. . . . It accepts no pinched dole of life. 'All the years,' it says, 'are mine. No age is shut against great intellects, no time is impenetrable to thought'."[7]

For authorities on his view of the soul, Traherne turned to the works attributed to "Hermes Trismegistus" and to Pico Della Mirandola's oration, *De Dignitate Hominis.* Traherne's debt to Hermes has been examined by Carol Marks in "Thomas Traherne and Hermes Trismegistus" (*RN*, XIX, 118-131) and in brief in other of her articles. Traherne quotes Hermes at length in *Christian Ethicks* to support his own contention that God's "Omnipresence and Eternity fill the Soul, and make it able to contain all Heights and Depths, and Lengths and Breadths whatsoever" (p. 227). He quotes Pico in the *Centuries* (IV, 74-78) illustrating the ability of human nature to become whatever it will, since the seeds of all possible lives are planted in it.

But nearly everything in Renaissance Platonism leads somehow to Ficino. As more and more is learned about Traherne, his relationship to Ficino appears all the stronger. S. Sandbank, in his article "Thomas Traherne on the Place of Man in the Universe," compares the philosophy of the nature of the soul espoused by Ficino with that of Traherne.[8] He finds in both the "Circulation Doctrine" which maintains "the human soul, knowing the lower in terms of the higher world, collects it, purifies it, and lifts it up to universality, thus restoring the unity of Being itself" (p. 122). Sandback cites Ficino's belief that the mind " ' can take on the spiritual forms of all things and become all' " (p. 126) and says that Traherne combines this theory of the mind transforming "things" into "thoughts" with the Aristotelian notion of thinking as "a transition from power to act" (p. 126). It should be noted however that the two theories of the working of the mind exist already in combination in Ficino who maintained, as Paul Oskar Kristeller points out, "The correspondence of the mind to an object consists in the fact that the mind brings from potentiality to actuality that particular one of its innate forms which corresponds to that particular object."[9] In Traherne the forms of the mind are not innate; but rather, they are created, a matter touched on later in this chapter.

The soul for Ficino, as for Traherne, is capable of becoming *omnia*, like God.

> Because the Soul is directed toward all truth and all good, and because in thinking and willing it attains some unity with its objects, it (the Soul) strives to become absolutely all, as God is all from all time.[10]

Ficino says that

> the entire effort of our Soul is to become God. This effort is as natural to man as that of flying is to birds. For it is inherent in all men, everywhere and always.[11]

In his emphasis on God as a Being who is Act, on God as both Potency and Act, in his postulation of Love and Knowledge as methods by which the soul mounts up to God, in his delineation of the ascent in terms of current psychology, in his classification of matter as devoid of Being except as it expresses Form, and in his devotion to Hermes, Ficino is the supreme example of the Renaissance Platonism which determines the course of Traherne's philosophy.

Platonic-Christian philosophy found its champions in seventeenth-century England in the group of thinkers known as the Cambridge Platonists. Traherne's debt to these men has been considered many times.[12] The latest and most authoritative study is by Carol Marks in "Thomas Traherne and Cambridge Platonism" (*PMLA*, LXXXI, 521-534). Marks finds Traherne most like Peter Sterry, among the Platonists, and notes that Sterry, Henry More, Nathaniel Culverwel and Traherne all make statements concerning the infinite capacity of the human soul (p. 529), though Marks does not feel Traherne was indebted to any of his contemporary Platonists for this idea. In the same line, Thompson, in his article on Traherne's philosophy, points to the Cambridge Platonist John Smith as one who, like Traherne, believes "the human mind by imitating God may gain 'the freedom of a true Eternity'."[13]

Because Traherne did not attend Cambridge, Carol Marks labels him an "Oxford Platonist" (p. 524). If we wanted to make a "school" of philosophy on this basis, we might begin by including Theophilus Gale and Robert South. Gale's system of reformed Platonism, which is developed primarily in the last part of *Court of the Gentiles*, does have its differences from Traherne's: on the nature of eternity and time, Gale adopts a position more truly Platonic, maintaining, so far as I can tell from Gale's garrulous prose, that there is an eternal "now" which is not like time but which, being one and the same thing with the Divine Being, may "comprehend" and "coexiste" with time though still not partaking in itself of the nature of succession (IV, 279-286). But in its assertions that the soul is of infinite capacity, Gale's philosophy is very congenial to Traherne's:

> From the spiritalitie of the Soul results its *infinite Capacitie*, of which *Plato* philosophiseth in his *Phaedrus*, pag. 245, 246.

> where he assimilates the Soul to a winged Chariot, which flies throughout the whole Universe. And what is the wing of the Soul, according to *Plato's* conception, but its innate and active capacitie of contemplating the supreme Truth, and persuing the last Good? . . . This infinite capacitie of the Soul ariseth from its immaterialitie: For by how much the lesse any subject partakes of mater and passive power, by so much the more Ample, Universal and Active is its capacitie. Things inanimate, yea Brutes, are therefore confined in their capacities, because they are wholly immersed in mater: God the supreme Being is most infinite; because a pure Act, altogether void of mater, yea al passive power. The human Soul, although it have an obediential passive power, as they phrase it, yet being not bound up by the Laws of Mater, it is invested with a capacitie of knowing and loving the most infinite Being. It's true, this capacitie of the human Soul is not *subjectively* and *actually* infinite, yet *objectively* and *potentially* it is. For such is the Benignite of God towards man, that he has implanted in his finite Nature an infinite capacitie, to take in and enjoy the first infinite Being. (II, 386-387)

This is taken from that part of Gale's work we know Traherne read.

Robert South, not really a philosopher, and a Platonist only
incidentally, in his sermon, "The Ways of Wisdom are Ways of
Pleasantness," speaks of the infinite power of the mind. The
mind is seen by him, as it is by Traherne, as a function of the
soul. It is, he says,

> a substance of a boundless comprehension. The mind of man
> is an image, not only of God's spirituality, but of his infinity.
> It is not like any of the senses, limited to this or that kind of
> object; as the sight intermeddles not with that which affects
> the smell; but, with a universal superintendence, it arbitrates
> upon and takes them all in. It is, as I may so say, an ocean,
> into which all the little rivulets of sensation, both external
> and internal, discharge themselves. It is framed by God to
> receive all, and more than nature can afford it; and so to be
> its own motive to seek for something above nature.
>
> (*Sermons*, I, 9)

South develops the theme of the infinite soul in his sermon, "Of
the Creation of Man in the Image of God," preached at St.
Paul's in 1662. Here he finds God's image to rest in the faculties
of the soul of man, in the understanding, the will, and the
passions or affections. South is not above including the body as
showing evidence of God's imprint as well, it being "a fit tabernacle for an immortal soul, not only to dwell in, but to contemplate upon" (I, 32).

Included in the "all" which can be contained in the soul is
eternity-time; most of Traherne's statements about the soul's
ability are concerned with this and, to a lesser extent, with the
perception of immensity and space. The *Theologia Germanica*
says that, like the soul of Christ,

> the created soul of man has also two eyes. The one is the
> power of seeing into eternity, the other of seeing into time
> and the creatures. . . . But these two eyes of the soul of man
> cannot perform their work at once. . . . Therefore whosoever
> will have the one must let the other go.[14]

But this would have been impossible for Traherne, for whom
the soul had but one eye, at times pictured as the "Infant-Ey,"
which sees the simultaneous existence of eternity-time.

So strangely glorious
    Hast thou made my Soul:
That even Yesterday is present
    To mine inward eye,
              (Infancy,
The days of my < Childhood,
              (Old Age.
    We have
    An endless Liberty.
    Being able to see, walk, be present there,
Where neither the Eagles eye, nor the Lions thought
can at all approach.
    The deeds of our Progenitors,
        Their Lives and Persons;
    Thy ways among the Ancients,
The services of the Sun in all Generations,
The Sun of Righteousness in his Rising and Eclipse;
    The Creation of the World,
    And the Government of Kingdoms,
        Can we behold;
    The day of Judgment,
    The Delights of Ages,
    The Sphere of time.
Nor will that contain us.
An infinite liberty we find beyond them;
    Can walk in thine Eternity,
        All at large;
    In every moment see it wholly,
        Know every where,
That from everlasting to everlasting thou art God;
Whose everlasting Glory is the Treasure of my Soul,
And thine eternal continuance a permanent
        NOW;
    With all its Contents
    For ever enjoyed.
          ("Thanksgivings for the Soul," 114-148)

This is, of course, how the soul exists in potential; in this world
it is often otherwise:

Men do mightily wrong themselvs: when they refuse to be
present in all Ages: and Neglect to see the Beauty of all
Kingdoms, and Despise the Resentments of evry Soul, and
Busie them selvs only with Pots and cups and things at home,

or shops and Trades and things in the street But do not liv to God Manifesting Himself in all the World. nor care to see, (and be present with Him, in) all the Glory of his Eternal Kingdom. By seeing the Saints of all Ages we are present with Them. By being present with them becom too Great for our own Age, and near to our Savior. (C, I, 85).

By knowing all things in time, the soul learns to extend itself so that it may go beyond the borders of time to all the eternity of which time is a part.

Having seen the general philosophical background, we may go on, then, to examine the religious and psychological grounds on which Traherne bases this theory of the Soul's ability to perceive eternity-time, concluding with a consideration of some special problems in this vein brought up by others who have discussed Traherne.

In *Christian Ethicks* Traherne deals at length with the problem of knowing the past and the future. In the chapters "Of Faith" and "Of Hope," he presents the groundwork of his method for raising the soul to its natural height of perception. Traherne compares the soul to Janus, a comparison which, as the editors of *Christian Ethicks* note, is found in Ficino and Pico; though, really, the idea of the two faces of the soul, according to Kristeller, goes back to Avicenna and Algazali.[15] Where Ficino's Janus looked with one face at eternity and the other at time, and the Janus of Pico symbolized the soul joining mind and body, Traherne carries the figure back to its earlier temporal significance and pictures it with one face directed toward the past, one toward the future. That face of the soul which sees the past Traherne calls "Faith," and the ability to see the future is named "Hope." With his characteristic and sometimes disconcerting ability to use an important term in more than one sense, Traherne also uses "Faith" to indicate the comprehensive nature of the soul which can include past, present and future within it. In these chapters, at least, Traherne states clearly that the word can have these two different meanings.

In incorporating these Christian virtues into his Platonic philosophy, Traherne makes it very clear that he finds in these concepts no measure of blind belief. Indeed, he says that Faith is the result of the perception of something tangible *outside* of the individual soul, not the uncovering of something innate within: "*Objects* of Faith are those Things which cannot be discovered but by the Testimony of others" (p. 107). The senses and reason may bring present things into the soul, but we know everything we do about the past because we have read it or been told about it. For knowledge of the past, Faith, we therefore turn to history; and the summary Traherne gives of the history of the world in "Of Faith" makes it clear that the history which really matters to him is that contained in the Bible and in the later documents of the Christian church. Though Traherne admits the possibility of false testimony in this history, he believes in the infallible ability of the reason, once it has sufficient information, to test and distinguish the true from the false. He lists a set of criteria by which the reason judges the testimony of history, including; compatibility with what we already know to be true, intrinsic consistency, lack of conflicting testimony, open publication, the existence of corroborating accounts, a long history of acceptance, references to other extant artifacts, prophecies and "types" anticipating the events recorded, purity of the doctrine contained within, and the ability of the knowledge gained to remove guilt and lead to felicity. "Now of all the Things that the World doth afford, the Christian Religion is that alone wherein all these Causes of Faith perfectly concur" (*CE*, p. 110). Even enemies of the religion accept as true its historical testimony.

It is partly because of this function of history in opening the past to the soul that the Bible plays such an important part in Traherne's system. Even the most casual reader of Traherne remembers his recounting of an early desire for a book from heaven, a book which he found to be already available to him as the Bible:

When the Bible was read my Spirit was present in other Ages. I saw the Light and Splendor of them: the Land of Canaan, the Israelites entering into it, the ancient Glory of the Amorites, their Peace and Riches, their Cities Houses Vines and Fig trees, the long Prosperity of their Kings, their Milk and Honie, their slaughter and Destruction, with the Joys and Triumphs of GODS People all which Entered into me, and GOD among them. I saw all and felt all in such a lively maner, as if there had been no other Way to those Places, but in Spirit only. This shewd me the Liveliness of

interior presence, and that all Ages were for most Glorious
Ends, Accessible to my Understanding, yea with it, yea within
it. for without changing Place in my self I could behold
and Enjoy all those. Any thing when it was proposed, tho
it was 10000 Ages agoe, being always before me.   (C, III, 24)

Obviously most modern readers would be reluctant to consider knowledge of the history of the Christian religion, primarily
as contained in the Bible, as "all things" in past time. But it
must be remembered that Traherne presents this merely as a
starting point. The Bible for him, as for Augustine, is seen as
the most reliable history available. Given the age in which he
lived, Traherne had little other choice or even a cause to look
elsewhere. We should remember Gale's *Court of the Gentiles*,
for instance, which tries to trace all language and philosophy
back to Hebraic, Biblical sources. Traherne's mind was by no
means uncritical; in *Roman Forgeries*, for instance, he labori-
ously attempts to demonstrate falsifications that have been
made in documents of the church. In Traherne's system, as
the soul begins to gain knowledge of reliable parts of history, this knowledge combines to form a whole which can
eventually become all of past time. "Where all these Things
meet together, they make a Foundation like that of the Great
Mountains which can never be moved" (*CE*, p. 110). And once
all time is seen, it will be seen to be glorious:

> Since all *Time* may be Objected to the Eye of Knowledge
> altogether, and Faith is prepared in the Soul on purpose, that
> all the Things in Time may be admitted into the Eye of
> the Soul, it is very Displeasing to Humane Reason, that *Time*
> should be horrid, and Dark, and empty, or that he that
> has expressed so much Love in the *Creation* of the World,
> should be Unmindful of our Concerns in the Dispensations of
> his *Providence*. Especially Since the World, how Glorious
> soever it is, is but the Theatre of more Glorious Actions, and
> the Capacity of *Time* as Great and Large as that of the
> *Universe*, Ages are as long and as Wide as Kingdoms.
> (CE, p. 111).

But the purpose of knowing the past is not merely to have the
knowledge for its own sake; by expanding the soul's vision
into the past we learn to direct the course of the future and even

to know what that future contains. In our individual human lives, we can appraise our present situation best through knowledge of our past life: "All a mans Life put together contributes a perfection to every part of it, and the Memory of things past is the most advantagious light of our present Condition" (CE, p. 212). And as to the Faith that "looks back upon Ages past: it takes in the Influences of all these, that it may bring forth fruit, in our Lives for the time to come" (CE, p. 115). Through Hope we know what will come. "Hope presupposes a Belief of the Certainty of what we desire" (CE, p. 117). The fact that prophecies have in the past been made and fulfilled assures us that other prophecies still to find their fulfillment will be realized. Here is where hope, in its more conventional sense, enters in; for there is in man a desire for all good things, for the "all" that God created good. This abundance of hope in the soul is the gift of prophecy, available to all men, for we could not possess these future things in our souls were they not already in being for us in some manner. Because we possess them in our souls, they are ours.

> Hope is for its Extent and Dimensions vast and wonderful. All the Honour, Advancement, Exaltation, Glory, Treasure, and Delight, that is concievable in Time or Eternity, may be hoped for: all that the Length, and Breadth, and Depth, and Height, of the Love of GOD, which passeth Knowledge, is able to perform; All that Ambition or Avarice can desire, all that Appetite and Self-Love can pursue, all that Fancy can imagine Possible and Delightful; Nay *more than we are able to ask or think*; we are able to desire, and aspire after (if it be promised to us) the very throne of GOD, and all the Joys of his Eternal Kingdom.   (CE, pp. 121-122)

These things, again, are certain. Traherne admits the possibility of "vicious" hopes; but presumably, since he believes in a hell where the suffering will be primarily mental, those whose hopes are evil will receive their vicious reward along with the burning knowledge of what they have lost.

The causes of Hope, like those of Faith, come originally to the soul from without, from reason and fancy acting upon sensory data. Yet as the soul begins its expansion in time, it stores up data; and gradually the process becomes tied less and less to the external senses and more to the "eye," the perceptive power, of the soul, until the soul becomes the prophetic spirit described by Ficino:

> Such a Soul by its nature is almost everywhere and always. It is not obliged to go outside itself in order to look at many and distant places and to recall the whole past and to antici-pate the future. Its achievements are won by leaving the body behind and by returning into itself, either because its nature is everywhere and always, as the Egyptians believe, or because when retiring into its own nature it is at once united with the divinity which includes all limits of places and times.[16]

Through Hope we can taste this future glory, but its fulfillment, according to Traherne, is only possible after death when the body is finally abandoned.[17]

> As by the Seed we conjecture what Plant will arise, and know by the Acorn what Tree will Grow forth, or by the Eagles Egge what Kind of Bird; so do we by the Powers of the Soul upon Earth, Know what kind of Being, Person, and Glory it will be in the Heavens. Its Blind and latent Powers shall be turned into Act, its Inclinations shall be completed, and its Capacities filled, for by this Means is it made Perfect. A Spiritual King is an Eternal Spirit. Lov in the Abstract is a Soul Exerted. Neither do you esteem yourself to be any other then LOV alone. GOD is Lov. And you are never like Him, till you are so: Lov unto all Objects in like manner. (C, IV, 70)

Love is the driving force of Faith and Hope; knowing and loving are almost one and the same and cannot exist in their true natures one without the other. Traherne constantly exhorts us to enjoy the world, to enjoy all, for joy is the fruit of love directed toward God's creation. Love is the concept which links all of Traherne's philosophy together. It is, as Sears Jayne says of love in Ficino's philosophy, the "key" to his system: "Ficino states it as a syllogism: everything is in God; God loves Himself; therefore, everything loves God. The motive force of the whole universe, then, is love."[18]
Readers of Traherne are affected more by the psychological development of an infinite soul as he describes it in terms of his own childhood than by his philosophical justification for the

concept, and understandably so. His descriptions of an infant's soul which knew no bounds are vivid and romantic. They strike a responsive chord, especially since modern psychology seems to have found a similar freedom from boundaries in the young child's psyche. Robert Ellrodt tries to trace the psychological genesis of Traherne's "obsession" for the infinite in *Les Poètes Métaphysiques Anglais*; but even he must ask of a part of Traherne's account, *"Souvenir d'enfance authentique?"* (I, ii, 341). Ellrodt does not seem to consider the answer too important. Yet we must take precautions against assuming Traherne's account of his childhood experience to be *in toto* autobiographical memories. If we, as readers, accept his theory of memory, we can say that Traherne has improved his soul's perception to the point where he is really able to remember the day he found himself "within / A House I knew not, newly clothd with Skin" ("The Preparative," 9-10). (This "House" is apparently the womb.) But even if this were so, Traherne, we must remember, is still using these childhood experiences in association with his philosophical position on the soul's infinity. These accounts, like all of his art, have a didactic purpose; and such a purpose must have its effect on how material is presented.

The real "message" of Traherne is not to return to the perception of childhood, or even to seek a mystic opening to eternity and immensity, but rather to improve the human faculties to the point where they become infinite and divine. As Robert Ellrodt says:

> La plus grande hardiesse de Traherne n'est pas de mettre en l'âme humaine l'intuition de l'infini, ce que Descartes eût approuvé ou seulement "l'image" de l'infinité divine, ce que la théologie traditionnelle eût accordé. C'est de prêter à l'homme des facultés infinies; mieux encore, d'en faire le centre et la circonférence de l'infinité, de cette infinité même qui serait l'essence éternelle de la Divinité.   (I, ii, 343)

Traherne's treatment of the soul's faculties is rather typical of Renaissance psychology. Through the number and names of the "faculties" the soul can have depends on whom you are reading in this period, and any one author is liable to be internally inconsistent, Edward Dowden, in "Elizabethan Psychology," published in 1907 in *Atlantic Monthly*, summarized the typical position:

It was generally agreed that the inner senses of the sensible
soul are three—reason, imagination or phantasy, and memory.
The brain consists of three cells, or ventricles, or wombs,—
each of these names was in common use,—and in each of
these one of the three faculties had its residence; each can,
however, pass on ideas to its neighbor faculty.

One should be aware that sometimes "faculties" refers to the
senses as well as to the more interior processes of
perception,—and sometimes not. The identification of three inner faculties was popular because this made the soul a trinity,
the image of God. "Understanding," could be substituted for
"reason" by some writers with no difference in meaning; but in
Crollius, for instance, the place of memory is taken by "mind,"
and mind is seen as something which encompasses the other two
faculties. This is reminiscent of Ficino who "lists among the
parts of the soul the *mens,* the *ratio,* the *idolum* and even the
body."[19] Traherne at one point uses a division that was popular
and had been used by Augustine: "Understanding, Will, and
Memory, which in the Soul are one, having thus an Impress of
the Trinity within it."[20] And in the same work Traherne also
speaks of the heart, understanding and memory in conjunction
so that "Will" might possibly be associated with "Hope" in the
heart, aligning it with imagination. The same sort of thing
occurs in Pierre Charron's *Of Wisdome,* which Traherne made
use of in *Christian Ethicks.* Charron identifies "three ventricles
before, wherein the reasonable soule doth exercise its faculties,
which are three, *Understanding, Memory, Imagination.*"[21] But
he later talks of the will as a function of the soul with a power
somewhat like that of imagination: "By the will . . . the soule
goeth foorth of it selfe, and lodgeth and liveth elsewhere in the
thing, beloved, into which it transformeth it selfe" (pp.
69-70). Edward Reynolds, whose *Treatise of the Passions and
Faculties of the Soule of Man* Traherne had read, identifies this
same power of going beyond all bounds with the imagination:
"For Reason, and all other powers, have their fixed and determined limits in Nature. . . . But the Imagination is a Facultie
boundlesse, and impatient of any imposed limits, save those
which it self maketh."[22]

The mind is the active power of the soul (*CE,* 231-232); and,
for all practical purposes, the two terms are synonymous in

Traherne. The presence of objects (eternity-time, immensity, created beings) in the mind or soul occurs through a process which Traherne calls "In-being" or "Indwelling." "For by the Indwelling of GOD all Objects are infused, and contained within" (*CE*, p. 73). The mind of a child is, according to Traherne, "a Rasa Tabula prepared in Him for the Drawing afterward of all the pictures in Gods kingdom" ("Select Meditations," IV, 2). That "all", as we have said, must come from without; and the process by which this "In-being" takes place is explained in Century I, 100. I quote it in full because the passage is a difficult one and has never been adequately explained:

> Christ Dwelling in our Hearts by Faith is an infinit Mystery. which may thus be understood. An Object Seen, is in the Faculty seeing it, and by that in the Soul of the Seer, after the Best of Maners. Whereas there are eight maners of In-being, the In-being of an Object in a Faculty is the Best of all. Dead Things are in a Room containing them in a vain maner; unless they are Objectivly in the Soul of a Seer. The Pleasure of an Enjoyer, is the very End why Things placed are in any Place. The Place and the Thing Placed in it, being both in the Understanding of a Spectator of them. Things Dead in Dead Place Effect nothing. But in a Living Soul, that seeth their Excellencies, they Excite a Pleasure answerable to their value, a Wisdom to Embrace them, a Courage not to Forsake them, a Lov of their Donor, Praises and Thanksgivings; and a Greatness and a Joy Equal to their Goodness. And thus all Ages are present in my Soul, and all Kingdoms, and GOD Blessed forever. And thus Jesus Christ is seen in me and dwelleth in me, when I believ upon Him. And thus all Saints are in me, and I in them. And thus all Angels and the Eternity and Infinity of GOD are in me for evermore. I being the Living TEMPLE and Comprehensor of them. Since therfore all other ways of In-being would be utterly vain, were it not for this: And the Kingdom of God (as our Savior saith, this Way) is within you; let us ever think and Meditat on Him, that His conception Nativity Life and Death may be always within us. Let Heaven and Earth Men and Angels, God and his Creatures be always within us. that is in our Sight, in our Sence, in our Lov and Esteem: that in the Light of the Holy Ghost we may see the Glory of His Eternal Kingdom, and Sing the Song of Moses, and the Song of the Lamb saying,

Great and Marvellous are thy Works Lord GOD Almighty,
Just and true are thy Ways Thou King of Saints.

The "eight maners of In-being" created a problem for H. M.
Margoliouth, editor of the *Centuries*. In the first printing of his
edition, he was forced to include a note reading, "This has
defeated me" (p. 253). In the 1965 reprint "from corrected
sheets of the first edition" this note is changed and directs
the reader to Aristotle's *Physics*, IV, iii. Here we find Aristotle
defining eight ways in which the word "in" may be used, including: the part "in" the whole, the whole "in" the part,
the species "in" the genus, etc.; but I fail to see how this has
anything to do with Traherne's statement. Traherne is not
talking about the definitions of "in," but about how an object
may come to dwell in a soul. According to this passage, the
object (any real entity) is perceived ("seen"); this perception
takes place "in" the faculty appropriate to the nature of the
object (objects of the past in the memory, etc.); and by being
"in" a faculty, that object is automatically "in" the soul. The
"eight maners of In-being" include, we read, "the In-being of an
Object in a Faculty." Assuming Traherne to be speaking of
the three faculties of the reasonable soul, this can happen in all
three of them, thus leaving five other methods of "In-being" to
be identified. Now since the object must be "seen," perceived,
in order to be in a faculty, as Traherne says, those five methods
must then be the five senses. We end up with a picture of the
soul much like Spenser's Castle of Alma in the second book of
the *Faerie Queene*.

The In-being of the faculties themselves in the soul does not
qualify as a ninth form because these faculties are part of and
one with the soul in a way that the senses, in relation to the
faculties, are not. Traherne's passage goes on to show that even
the In-dwelling of Christ comes originally from sensory data,
though knowledge of Christ has value not as it is to the sense
perception but as it exists once it is in the soul. Could Indwelling in the faculties of the soul not take place, "all other
ways of In-being," and I think here again he is referring to the
five senses, "would be utterly vain." Though Traherne is not
always content to divide the soul into only three parts, here at
least he seems to be using that system of the faculties. The soul's
objects stand in regard to the soul just as matter does to act.

The soul, like God, is act; things have value only as they exist in an act. Because of the infinite capacity of the three faculties of the soul, all things are open to them, in time, as acts.

Throughout his work Traherne not only talks of the infinite capacity of the soul in general but also dwells, especially, on the infinity of one particular faculty, the understanding or reason:

> [Man's] Understanding is an endless Light, and can infinitly be present in all Places, and see and Examine all Beings, survey the reasons, surmount the Greatness, exceed the Strength, contemplat the Beauty, Enjoy the Benefit, and reign over all it sees and Enjoys like the Eternal GODhead.   (C, II, 23)

"The true exemplar of GODS infinity is that of your Understanding, which is a lively Patern and Idea of it. It excludeth Nothing, and containeth all Things" (C, II, 24). The understanding is of such importance because it is by knowledge of present objects that we know the past and anticipate the future. The soul is "by its Understanding a Temple of Eternity, and GODS Omnipresence" (C, II, 70).

The operations, the acts of the understanding and of the other faculties are termed "thoughts" by Traherne. "GOD hath made it Easy to convert our Soul into a Thought containing Heaven and Earth" (C, II, 87). One starts with "things," but as he grows in spirit he finds the thoughts created of much greater importance. When Traherne asks:

> Did I grow, or did I stay?
> Did I prosper or decay?
>   When I so
> From *Things* to *Thoughts* did go?
> Did I flourish or diminish,
> When I so in *Thoughts* did finish
> What I had in *Things* begun;
> When from God's Works to think upon
> The Thoughts of Men my Soul did com?
>   ("The Review I," 1-9)

the answer is no surprise. "Compar'd to them, / I *Things* as *Shades* esteem" (18-19). The same view is expressed in the poem, "Dreams" (50-56):

> Thought! Surely *Thoughts* are tru;
> They pleas as much as *Things* can do:
> Nay Things are dead,
> And in themselvs are severed
> From Souls; nor can they fill the Head
> Without our Thoughts.   Thoughts are the Reall things
> From whence all Joy, from whence all Sorrow springs.

The reader must beware of pausing too long at the end of the second to last line, taking the play on words too seriously. Traherne is in no way impinging the reality of "Things" but merely showing, as he does so often, that things without participation in act are utterly without value. It is in the poems entitled "Thoughts" that the power of these mental operations to enter all space and time is perhaps best portrayed:

> The Ey's confind, the Body pent
> In narrow Room: Lims are of small Extent.
> But Thoughts are always free.
> And as they're best,
> So can they even in the Brest,
> Rove ore the World with Libertie:
> Can Enter Ages, Present be
> In any Kingdom, into Bosoms see.
> Thoughts, Thoughts can come to Things, and view,
> What Bodies cant approach unto.
> They know no Bar, Denial, Limit, Wall:
> But have a Liberty to look on all.
>   ("Thoughts. I," 61-72)

> Thoughts are the Wings on which the Soul doth flie,
> The Messengers which soar abov the Skie,
> Elijahs firey Charet, that conveys
> The Soul, even here, to those Eternal Joys.
> Thoughts are the privileged Posts that Soar
> Unto his Throne, and there appear before
> Our selvs approach. These may at any time
> Abov the Clouds, abov the Stars may clime.
> The Soul is present by a Thought; and sees
> The New Jerusalem, the Palaces,
> The Thrones and feasts, the Regions of the Skie,
> The Joys and Treasures of the DEITIE.
> His Wisdom makes all things so Bright and pure,

That they are worthy ever to endure.
His Glorious Works his Laws and Counsels are,
When seen, all like himself, beyond compare.
All Ages with his Love and Glory Shine,
As they are his all Kingdoms are Divine.
("Thoughts. IV," 1-18)

Thus the soul or mind is at birth an empty vessel infinite in capacity. It exists without temporal or spatial limits or bounds. Through the senses, however, the soul begins to take in the world around it; and impulses from the senses come to be lodged in the faculties of the soul where they exist as thoughts. The ignorant soul places more emphasis on sense perception than on thoughts and comes to believe itself limited, bound in space and time. But as he learns more, as his thoughts develop, he sees the value of things really to lie in their presence in his mind. As he turns from things to thoughts, the soul discovers that with these he is able to transcend the limits of space and time and to be present everywhere always. Although the full realization of this power is possible only after death, the soul on this earth, through the study of history and of the eternal things in the present (such as the body's form and the services of the world), expands its vision toward the infinite perception of God of whom it is the image.

Frances Yates, in her work on the Renaissance art of memory, (see bibliography) has shown the belief in the unlimited power of thought to be a primary Hermetic concept on which occult memory magic rested. Though it would be presumptuous to call this occult art a "corruption" of the Neo-Platonic concept, it should at least be noted that Traherne, unlike Ficino and Henry More, did not, so far as we know, allow his metaphysics to lead him to magic. The systematic study of history discussed in this chapter and the meditative practice outlined in the next are not at all occult. They do not depend on physical objects of association but are, after the initial sensory learning process, intellectual operations. The operation of the mind in these exercises is explained by Traherne on as rational grounds as he is able to find; there is no leap, unless it might be the leap of death, with which one suddenly knows all. The only thing to make this appear "supernatural" to us is the degree to which Traherne believed the learning process could be carried, but this in itself does not make the process an occult or magic one. The objects we are to contemplate are not important only as symbols but are the very things of memory. If Traherne sees the world in his mind, he sees it not as a reference system into which to fit daily experience in order to remember it, but as the world, God's creation, a thing to be known and loved in itself.[23]

Traherne's philosophy of the operation of the mind as it perceives past, present and future has been compared to that of St. Augustine by Louis Martz in *The Paradise Within*. Martz begins by giving an account of Augustine's concept of time-perception which, though not specifically applied to Traherne, is more true of Traherne than it is of Augustine. Augustine, according to Martz, believes that "the mind can in some measure transcend the oppressive transience of time, and act as an image of God's timeless mind, in which all things have their simultaneous existence" thus "enabling the mind to act as a mirror of eternity" (p. 52). Martz quotes from Book 11 (Chapters 9, 20 and 28) of the *Confessions,* apparently to support his contention; but the whole point of these quoted passages and of the entire discussion of time in the *Confessions* is to show that the human mind *cannot* perceive the past and the future because these things do not even exist so far as the mind is concerned. Nearly all commentators on Augustine agree in this interpretation of the discussion. Augustine, according to Ronald Suter:

contends that just because facts are related about the past, this does not mean that we must now discern things which are past. For instance, the image of an adult's childhood can be present in the adult's memory without his childhood itself being present at the time he recalls it. Thus the fact that we can talk about the past in no way proves its existence.[24]

Martz quotes this from Augustine:

Clear now it is and plain, that neither things to come, nor things past, are. Nor do we properly say, there be three times, past, present, and to come; but perchance it might be properly said, there be three times: a present time of past things; a present time of present things; and a present time of future things. For indeed three such as these in our soul there be.   (*Confessions,* XI, 20; quoted p. 53)

Yet Augustine, as John J. Callahan points out, says "not only that whatever exists is present, though it may appear to be past, but also that what exists is not the past event itself but only an image of it."[25] As to the future, according to Augustine it is utterly unknowable to the ordinary human soul though it may, nevertheless, be anticipated from things in the present:

> Future things then are not yet and if they be not yet, they are not: and if they are not, they cannot be seen; yet foretold they may be from things present, which are already and are seen.[26]

Though Augustine has much to say of the great capacity of the memory, he nevertheless maintains that

> when past facts are related, there are drawn out of the memory, not the things themselves which are past, but words which, conceived by the images of things, they, in passing, have through the senses left traces in the mind. (p. 257)

These "traces in the mind" are a long way from the timeless perception of the Deity. Augustine's system is fundamentally different from Traherne's in that Traherne believes the past or future act perceived by the soul to be that act itself as it endures in eternity; Augustine firmly denies this, saying man can see only the present, a present which cannot include past or future. As a result of his comparison, Martz finds Traherne's *Centuries* stressing primarily the present, though still employing memory and expectation as devices. Martz fails to see how the *Centuries* use past, present and future to recreate the timeless all of Eternity. In Traherne, all three of these parts of time are equally important, equally perceptible, and equally real; for, in essence, they are one.

We should not conclude this consideration of Traherne's philosophy of perception without comment on the soul's vision of "infinite space," if only because this has previously been of so much critical interest. There are important treatments of the subject by Marjorie Hope Nicolson in *The Breaking of the Circle*, by Rosalie L. Colie in both *Paradoxia Epidemica* and her earlier article, "Thomas Traherne and the Infinite," and by Carol Marks in "Thomas Traherne and Cambridge Platonism." Nicolson and especially Colie attribute Traherne's "*passion de l'infini*" to the "New Science"; however, as Ellrodt points out:

Sans doute le sens de l'infini se serait-il affirmé de manière moins concrète, moins cosmique, dans le cadre rigide de l'univers ptolémaïque. Mais rien n'assure que la passion êut été moins forte.   (I, ii, 335)

Traherne accepted the idea of the possibility of infinite extension, infinite space, but did not see it as identical with the infinite, presence of God, a fact Carol Marks places beyond doubt in her article, quoting from Traherne's attack in his "Commonplace Book" upon Henry More's theory of the identity of infinite space and divine omnipresence (*PMLA*, LXXI, 529-30). Traherne did, however, find "infinite space" within the human soul; and it was there that the omnipresence of God was imaged. We should beware of confusing these extensions. The infinity within is larger than the infinity without and can include, can "comprehend" it (*C*, V, 2).

One would think that beside infinit Space there could be no more Room for any Treasure. yet to shew that God is infinitly infinit, there is Infinit Room besides, and perhaps a more Wonderfull Region making this to be infinitly infinit.   No man will believ that besides the Space from the Centre of the Earth to the utmost bounds of the Everlasting Hills, there should be any more.   Beyond those Bounds perhaps there may, but besides all that Space that is illimited and present before us, and absolutly endles evry Way, where can there be any Room for more?   (*C*, V, 6)

Where is the place that can hold infinite space? Traherne goes on to tell: "This is the Space that is at this Moment only present before our Ey, the only Space that was, or that will be, from Everlasting to Everlasting." Only the interior, the perceived infinity is eternal. Traherne concludes this section of the Fifth Century with a transition to the subject of eternity, a shift which provides another example of his use of spatial analogy to explain that concept:

This Moment Exhibits infinit Space, but there is a Space also wherein all Moments are infinitly Exhibited, and the Everlasting Duration of infinit Space is another Region and Room of Joys. Wherein all Ages appear together, all Occurrences stand up at once, and the innumerable and Endless

Myriads of yeers that were before the Creation, and will be after the World is ended are Objected as a Clear and Stable Object, whose several Parts extended out at length, giv an inward Infinity to this Moment, and compose an Eternitie that is seen by all Comprehensors and Enjoyers.

Thus, for Traherne, space was no more infinite than time. If space is infinite, it is not as infinite as the omnipresence of God which has an interior presence within the soul, a "place" where not only infinite space may be perceived but much, much more. The justification of this inclusion of an infinite within an infinite is the nature of the human mind which may conceive of infinite space and yet may conceive of something in addition to it, above it, and greater than it. That of which no greater can be conceived is God.[27] The "space" important to Traherne was seen without a telescope, just as time in his philosophy did not depend upon the invention of the clock. Eternity-time is the existence of the world in the divine eternity; infinite space, of the creation in spiritual immensity.

The Renaissance was the age of the rediscovery of history. The modern age, which dawned in the seventeenth century, is a discovery of the nature of the present moment, of the universe as it is to the senses and to our mechanical extensions of the senses. Modern eyes have become directed much more toward the empty vacuity beyond our atmosphere than they have been backward along the line of human history or forward to the future results of present actions. Though modern critics have found Traherne's ideas about infinite space of interest, the infinity really important to Traherne was a spiritual one. Traherne was not a "modern" man. While surely he would have made no distinction between the importance of God's eternity and His immensity, in his philosophy the important continuum for humanity is nonetheless that of eternity-time. It is in time that our actions both take place and are forever preserved, actions for which we eternally pay the consequences.

NOTES

1. IV (London, 1677), 291. According to Carol Marks, Traherne extracts portions of Part II (Oxford, 1670; I use the London edition of 1676 in the following) in the "Commonplace Book." He also includes passages from this part of Gale's work in the "Ficino Notebook." Parts III and IV of *Court of*

56   THE TEMPLE OF ETERNITY

the Gentiles were not published in Traherne's lifetime. On Traherne and
Gale see Marks, "Thomas Traherne's Commonplace Book," *PBSA,* LVIII,
458-465, and "Traherne's Ficino Notebook," *PBSA,* LXIII, 73-81, as well as
the introduction and notes to the Marks and Guffey edition of *Christian
Ethicks.* One cannot help wondering, with James M. Osborn, if the "T.G."
addressed in the "Select Meditations," II, 38 is not Gale (see "A New
Traherne Manuscript," *TLS,* Oct. 8, 1964, p. 928). In a 1917 article, J. W.
Proud suggested that Traherne had written "some anonymous laudatory
poems prefixed to Parts I and II of Theophilus Gale's great work, The
Court of the Gentiles" ("Thomas Traherne: A Divine Philosopher,"
Friends Quarterly Examiner, no. 201, p. 66). There seems to be no evidence
for this; and, in spite of the fact that one poem does use an image
important in Traherne, the reflecting pool of water, it seems unlikely that
Traherne would use it in such a negative way:
"Thus with dejected Eye
  In standing pools we seek the skie:
    To find the milkie way,
    Not only lose the day:
    But down to Caverns, and vast tracts of night
    Go to improve the sight."
                                                    (II, b2ᵛ)
Gale was at Oxford, as student, then as tutor, from 1647-1660.
  2. See "Select Meditations," II, 94.
  3. See *CE,* p. 182.
  4. *SP,* LXV, 86. The italics are his.
  5. In *Psychodia Platonica.* (Cambridge, 1642) On even More's recognition of this as a dead issue, see C. A. Staudenbaur, "Galileo, Ficino and
Henry More's *Psychathanasia,*" *Journal of the History of Ideas,* XXIX
(1968), 575.
  6. *Spiritual Reformers,* p. 328.
  7. *Seneca's Letters to Lucilius,* trans. E. Phillips Barker, II, 197-198.
  8. *Studies in English Language and Literature,* ed. Alice Shalvi and A. A.
Mendilow (Jerusalem, 1966), pp. 121-136.
  9. *The Philosophy of Marsilio Ficino,* trans. Virginia Conant, p. 51.
  10. Kristeller, pp. 117-118.
  11. *Opera Omnia,* p. 305 quoted in Kristeller, p. 337.
  12. Some of these considerations are: T. O. Beachcroft, "Traherne and
the Cambridge Platonists," Gertrude R. Sherer, "More and Traherne,"
Frances L. Colby, "Traherne and the Cambridge Platonists: An Analytical
Comparison," as well as "Thomas Traherne and Henry More," and Elbert
N. S. Thompson, "The Philosophy of Thomas Traherne;" see bibliography.
  13. P. 105. The quotation of Smith is taken from E. T. Campagnac, *The
Cambridge Platonists* (Oxford, 1905), p. 123.
  14. Trans. Susanna Winkworth, p. 124.
  15. P. 197 n. Kristeller refers the reader to Marian Heitzman, "L'agostin-
ismo avicennizzante e il punto di partenza della filosofia di Marsilio
Ficino," *Giornale Critico Della Filosofia Italiana,* XVI (1935), 298, 321.
  16. *Opera Omnia,* p. 288 quoted in Kristeller, p. 312.
  17. See the discussion of Glory in the next chapter.
  18. *Marsilio Ficino's Commentary on Plato's Symposium* (Columbia,
Missouri, 1944), p. 24.
  19. Sears R. Jayne, *John Colet and Marsilio Ficino* (Oxford, 1963),
p. 57.
  20. *Meditations on the Six Days of the Creation,* p. 83.

THE TEMPLE OF ETERNITY

21. *Of Wisdome Three Bookes,* trans. Samson Lennard (London, 1606),
p. 46.
22. (London, 1640), p. 24. See Marks, "Traherne's Early Studies," *PBSA,*
LXII (1968), 511-536.
23. It is ironic that one of the few bits of biographical information we
have about Traherne records two "psychic" experiences, though hardly
spectacular ones:
"Mr. Traherne, B.D. (chaplain to Sir Orlando Bridgman, Lord Keeper), a
learned and sober person, was son of a shoemaker in Hereford; one night
as he lay in bed, the moon shining very bright, he saw the phantom of
one of the apprentices sitting in a chair in red waistcoat and headband
about his head, and strap upon his knee, which apprentice was really
in bed and asleep with another fellow-apprentice, in the same chamber,
and saw him. The fellow was living, 1671. Another time, as he was in
bed, he saw a basket sailing in the air, along by the valence of his bed; I
think there was fruit in the basket; it was a phantom. From himself."
(Aubrey's "Miscellanies" [1696], quoted in Margoliouth, I, xxviii-xxix.)
However, concern with this sort of supernatural occurrence is far from
characteristic of the Traherne we know through his own poetry and prose.
24. "Augustine on Time with Some Criticisms from Wittgenstein," *Revue
Internationale de Philosophie,* XVI (1962), 382.
25. *Four Views of Time in Ancient Philosophy,* (Cambridge, Mass.,
1948), p. 156.
26. *Confessions,* (Modern Library Ed.), p. 258.
27. See Traherne's poem, "Misapprehension," 1.27.

IV

Types and Shadows

Together with his stress on the study of history, Traherne presents a meditative practice which functions through an ordered contemplation upon the similarities of historical events. Again, these events are drawn from the most reliable of histories, the Bible, as well as from that other reliable source of information about things in eternity-time, personal experience. Along the lines of traditional exegetical practice, persons and events in history are seen by Traherne as "types" or "shadows" of parallel persons and events following them in time. They are also seen as representatives of spiritual states or conditions. The purpose of this mode of thinking is the same as that of the study of history: to make the human soul more like the Divine Being. For, just as events in the Old Testament foreshadowed and promised the coming of the Messiah, so His life, death and resurrection speak to us of our own return to the divine nature, a return which is brought about through the imitation of Christ.

The major events of history form a pattern which is repeated in the life of Christ and in individual human lives. Thus Adam in Eden, the world after the Fall, Christ Incarnate and Christ Glorified become figures for the stages of human experience in the march toward God as Traherne identifies them: Innocence, Misery, Grace and Glory. In Traherne's system there is thus a means to reconcile the classical view of time as cyclical with the Christian idea of a linear time progression leading to the Last Judgment. Traherne's universe is a universe of mirrors. Time in eternity shares the stable nature of eternity for two reasons: (1) as already pointed out in the second chapter, it is all in existence at once and thus cannot change, and (2) many of its

58

parts are alike; what follows any of the major points of division on the line is a repetition, with variations, of what precedes that point. To avoid over-simplification, however, it should be noted that there is an increasing superiority of value as events lead toward the end of time.

Traherne's major parallels were those already well established in the body of knowledge known as "typology." "Typology," says Jean Daniélou, "is the study of correspondences between the Old and the New Testaments."[1] Were it only as simple as that statement makes it seem. For hundreds of years, Christian writers have argued about what "parallels" are and are not types. For three hundred years, at least, theologians have attempted to make a distinction between true types and those which are the product of allegorizing.

In the seventeenth century, Benjamin Keach attempted to define rigid distinctions between types and allegories. The main distinction he made was that types deal with two historical persons or "facts," while allegories are doctrinal, illustrating some moral content. When he comes, however, to list those things he regards as types, Keach ignores his own distinctions, so much that he is able to deal, for instance, with the circumcision as a type of "the cutting off the Lusts of the Heart and Life." (*Tropes and Figures*, pt. 1, p. 433).

Nineteenth and twentieth-century commentators have stressed the points that typological comparisons teach a higher truth than either half could have communicated alone, that they deal with real circumstances rather than with fictional ones, and that they were intended by God to be parallel and are not merely the product of human ingenuity (revelation being the necessary proof for this).[2] In addition, typology, now as in the past, is carried beyond simple Old Testament-New Testament comparisons to include applications of Biblical types to antitypes in the history of the church and to "the life of each individual soul, as *alter Christus*" (Daniélou, p. 215).

All of this makes "typology" a very uncertain term. Faced with this problem of definition, William G. Madsen, in his book *From Shadowy Types to Truth: Studies in Milton's Symbolism*, makes the point that Milton was not specifically involved in determining typological relationships. "The relevance of the theory of typology to Milton's poetry lies in the fact that Milton employed typology not as a dictionary

of ready-made symbols but as a mode of discourse" (p. 6).
The same thing might be said of Traherne. Not himself directly concerned in the theological exegesis of types, he has,
rather, a habit of thought which makes constant use of spiritual
parallels. Madsen, however, feels a need for a means of differ-
entiating typology from allegory, metaphor, etc.; he sets down a
list of criteria he believes Milton's contemporaries used in determining types. Study of seventeenth-century works on figures and
types, however, reveals exceptions to nearly every one.[3]

Considering, then, the vagueness of typology as a term and as
a method of exegesis, and taking into account the limits of our
purpose here, it seems wiser not to proceed to a further statement of definition. Instead, for the purposes of this study, let us
say that in Traherne's works there are expressed and implied
comparisons of important persons, places and events, comparisons which have historically been called "typological." In these
comparisons, the type has the function of foreshadowing the
antitype. These typologies include the relationships of Adam to
Christ, David to Christ, and Eden to the New Jerusalem. Beyond this, it can be said that Traherne employed a method of
thought which was constantly finding parallels between the Old
and New Testament, between the history of the world and the
history of the individual, and between God and man,—call that
method "typology" or what you will.

Traherne speaks of "types" several times in *Christian Ethicks.*
In the chapter "Of Repentance" occurs what Marks and
Guffey call "an exercise in typology" (p. 342n.). Here Traherne
finds his subject "fitly Typified in the old Law, by the Laver
that was set at the Door of the Tabernacle for the Priests to
wash in, before they entred into the Sanctuary" (p. 129); and
the comparison of the temple is developed at length. This
passage does contain some comparisons of which both parts are
tangible objects such as those of the altar which "answers our
Saviors Cross" and the veil "of *Rams-skins* died *Red,* to signifie
the Blood of Christ" (p. 129). But most of the things mentioned have a moral or spiritual antitype and are what today
might be called "figures." Traherne would not have accepted
the modern judgment that both halves of a "typological" comparison must be historical.

For an understanding of the use Traherne makes of Adam,
David and Christ in his writing, we must view these individuals

ι the typological framework that had developed around
Both Adam and David were taken as types of Christ. The
;-Christ typology, however it may have originated, goes
for most Christians to two statements by Paul, one in I.
5:

> And so it is written: The first man Adam was made a
> living soule, the last Adam was made a quickening spirit.
> . Howbeit that was not first which is spirituall: but that
> which is naturall, and afterward that which is spirituall.
> . The first man is of the earth, earthy: The second man is
> the Lord from heaven.
> }. As is the earthy, such are they that are earthy, and as is
> the heavenly, such are they also that are heavenly.
>). As we have borne the image of the earthly, wee shall also
> beare the image of the heavenly.[4]

ε other passage referring to Adam as a type is Rom. 5:14:
:vertheles, death reigned from Adam to Moses, even over
ιn that had not sinned after the similitude of Adams trans-
ιsion, who is the figure of him that was to come." These
ame primary loci for the study of the typology in spite of the
ι that in the comparison, to quote R. M. Grant, in The
'ter and the Spirit, "the correspondence is not as important as
ε difference."
Chief credit for the propagation and development of this
ιology after Paul belongs to St. Irenaeus and his work Against
ιresies, a book with which Traherne was familiar, as is
idenced in Roman Forgeries.[5] Both Paul and Irenaeus extend
ιe typology to what Daniélou would call its "mystical"
ιterpretation, its application to the individual Christian. That
l mankind is included in Adam was a Rabbinic doctrine that
ιd become traditional by the time Paul wrote.[6] Irenaeus ex-
ιnds this to maintain that Christ, by saving man in general,
ιso saved the first Adam:

> Adam [is] the first formed man, of whom the Scripture says
> that the Lord spake, "Let Us make man after Our own image
> and likeness;" and we are all from him: and as we are
> from him, therefore have we all inherited his title. But in-
> asmuch as man is saved, it is fitting that he who was created
> the original man should be saved.[7]

The David-Christ comparison had received significant consideration by Augustine:

> We have, in fact, found Jesus Christ explicitly called David by the Prophet Ezeckiel. . . . The Prophet Osee, too, when he foretold the state of the Jews in which they now are, prophesied also that afterwards they would believe in Christ, that same Christ under the name of David.[8]

The important points for comparison between Adam and Christ were that both came directly from God without another father, that Adam was God's image as Christ was his son, and that Christ regained what Adam had lost, Paradise. The important comparison between David and Christ is that both were God's chosen kings. And just as Adam's Paradise foreshadowed the Paradise to come after the Redemption, so, according to Augustine, "In the progress of the city of God through the ages, therefore, David first reigned in the earthly Jerusalem as a shadow of that which was to come." Even the songs that David sang, his Psalms, have a place in the comparison: "For the rational and well-ordered concord of diverse sounds in harmonious variety suggests the compact unity of the well-ordered city."[9] Adam was a type of Christ Incarnate; the Fall was a type, though in reverse, of Christ Crucified; David was a type of Christ Glorified, of Christ the King.

In addition to this tradition of Old Testament-New Testament typology, there was another important tradition related to it that we must note, one indicated in the title of Thomas A'Kempis' great work, *The Imitation of Christ*. Bertram Dobell, in his edition of *Centuries of Meditations*, recognized a parallel purpose in these two works, in each of which "the writer . . . declares his object to be the setting up of a Light whereby the life of man may be guided and ruled in accordance with the will of God" (p. *xx*). Dobell finds Traherne to be writing in the tradition of the *Imitation* and does an admirable job of comparing and contrasting the qualities of the two works. The two books are certainly very different in many respects, and one could imagine that the apparent anti-intellectualism of the *Imitation* would have grated on a man of such learning as Traherne. Yet the idea which is the major point of similarity, that the Christian imitates in his own life

the life of Christ, seems inseparable from the whole of the
Christian religion and not something, like a particular typology,
that can be traced along a line of development apart from
the total history of Christian doctrine.

One final, traditional comparison must necessarily be treated
in order to follow Traherne's delineation of the progress of the
soul; that is the analogy between the history of the world and
the growth of the individual. Traherne accepted the Christian
idea of history, that it is a linear progression leading the world
toward the Last Judgment and thus back to the perfection from
which it fell. He must also have been aware of the tradition of
regarding this growth of the world as a progress from infancy
to maturity. Ronald Crane treats the background of this idea in
his article, "Anglican Apologetics and The Idea of Progress,
1699-1745," and points out that:

> Tertullian, as early as the beginning of the third century, had
> likened the history of religion to a gradual process of
> education, with stages of growth comparable to those of an
> individual's life from infancy to maturity; just as everything
> in nature, he declared, reaches its perfection by successive
> steps, so the divine truth, though in itself one and unchang-
> ing, is communicated to men progressively in time and is
> adapted in each stage to their capacities and needs.[10]

Crane finds examples of the same comparison in Augustine, in
Vincent of Lerins and in Thomas Aquinas.

In Traherne's system, as the mind takes in the history of the
world it sees that this history parallels its own individual
growth; indeed, the soul can actually experience past and future
time because of the nature of this correspondence. The
history of the world, the life of Christ, the progress of the soul:
these three parallel movements are what the soul comes to see as
its vision is expanded. Because of the similarities, it comes
to know the first two movements not simply intellectually but,
in its own experience of growth, experiences all growth. In the
soul, past and future acts may exist with the same degree of
reality as immediate experience. To see the innocence of childhood is to see Adam in Paradise; to see yourself growing daily
in the spirit of God is to see the movement of history itself.
Things are many; acts, operations abstracted from their causes,
are few. Acts are what abide forever in eternity-time.

Traherne divides the act of growth into four stages, which he terms "estates."[11] These states of existence he names Innocence, Misery, Grace and Glory. Marks and Guffey remark that, "The classification occurs in other writers of the period" (*CE*, p. 307n.) citing John Bartlet's *The Practical Christian*, which briefly proposes a similar, though not identical, four-part system for meditation. The editors go on to say, "The usual arrangement was tripartite." Though Marks and Guffey take no note of it, it would seem that Traherne himself at times regards the division as one into three parts, combining Misery and Grace into one estate. In the passage from *Christian Ethicks* to which the above note is appended, Traherne says that among the things he will speak of in this work are "What Vertues belong to the Estate of *Innocency*, what to the Estate of *Misery* and *Grace*, and what to the Estate of *Glory*" (p. 4). The two are grouped together again in a discussion of virtue in "Select Meditations" III, 53 (quoted *CE*, p. 317n.). In one treatment, Misery is left out altogether (*CE*, pp. 29-30) and in several places the estate of "Trial" appears to have been substituted for Misery and Grace (*CE*, pp. 112-113, 167-168, 184).

The two estates of Misery and Grace tend to combine, I believe, because in the world they represent a transitional state and are themselves usually found in combination. In the history of the individual soul, of Christ and of the world, there is never a period so miserable as to be devoid of all grace, nor so full of grace as not to have something to hold it to its earthly condition—otherwise, it would enter glory. All four estates have areas in which they overlap, but none so much as Misery and Grace. This is best illustrated in *Century*, III, 43, the key passage for any discussion of Traherne's estates, where Traherne catalogs the things he associates with each one:

In the Estate of Innocency we are to Contemplate the Nature and Maner of [man's] Happiness, the Laws under which He was governed, the Joys of Paradice, and the Immaculat Powers of His Immortal Soul. In the Estate of Misery we hav his Fall the Nature of Sin Original and Actual, His Manifold Punishments Calamity Sickness Death &c. In the Estate of Grace; the Tenor of the New Covenant, the maner of its Exhibition under various Dispensations of the Old and New Testament, the Mediator of the Covenant, the Conditions of it Faith and Repentance, the Sacraments or Seals of it, the

Scriptures Ministers and Sabbaths, the Nature and Govern-
ment of the Church, its Histories and Successions from the
Beginning to the End of the World. &c. In the State of Glory;
the Nature of Separat Souls,[12] their Advantages Excellen-
cies and Privileges, the Resurrection of the Body, the Day of
Judgment and Life Everlasting.

From this it can be seen that many of the things listed under
Misery and Grace occur intermingled all along the time line of
history, while those things associated with Innocence and Glory
are either purely spiritual (as opposed to historical) or occupy a
definite place at the beginning or end of universal and individual history.

Innocence, as the above passage from the *Centuries* shows, is a
state associated with a pre-Fall world, with man's ideal condition of happiness and spiritual power. In the life of the
individual, it is the state of childhood, before the infant is
tainted by the world, a condition which we so often find sung
about with joy in Traherne. The child comes into the world
like Adam and Christ:

> Long time before
> I in my Mothers Womb was born,
> A GOD preparing did this Glorious Store,
> The World for me adorne.
> Into this Eden so Divine and fair,
> So Wide and Bright, I com his Son and Heir.
>   ("The Salutation," 31-36)

The world of the child is a paradise not solely because of what
is in it, but also because of what the child does not see:

> Harsh ragged Objects were conceald,
>   Oppressions Tears and Cries,
> Sins, Griefs, Complaints, Dissentions, Weeping Eys,
>   Were hid: and only Things reveald,
> Which Heav'nly Spirits, and the Angels prize.
>   The State of Innocence
> And Bliss, not Trades and Poverties,
>   Did fill my Sence.
>   ("Wonder," 25-32)

Only what Adam in his first Estate,
    Did I behold.
            ("Eden," 29-30)

We meditate on Adam and the state of childhood in order to
find the true, original nature of man and the world. Infancy
teaches the adult:

All Bliss
Consists in this,
    To do as *Adam* did;
And not to know those superficial Joys
    Which were from him in *Eden* hid.
            ("The Apostacy," 37-41)

To Infancy, O Lord, again I com,
    That I my Manhood may improv:
    My early Tutor is the Womb;
        I still my Cradle lov.
            ("The Return," 1-4)

But Wantonness and Avarice got in. . . .
    And all my Pleasure was in Sin:
Who had at first with simple Infant-Eys
Beheld as mine ev'n all Eternities.
            ("An Infant-Ey," 37, 46-48)

The infant has a sense, sometimes imaged as an "Ey," which
is dimmed considerably if not blotted out as he grows older, but
which can in its pure state perceive eternity and infinity:

. . . but I
Forgot the rest, and was all Sight, or Ey.
    Unbodied and Devoid of Care,
Just as in Heavn the Holy Angels are.
        For Simple Sence
Is Lord of all Created Excellence.
            ("The Preparative," 35-40)

This "Simple Sence" is an interior presence, the *tabula rasa* on
which ideas are later written.
    Two topics concerning Traherne and childhood, though
treated often before, must be taken into account. These are

original sin and pre-existence (existence of the soul before
birth). It seems obvious that Traherne believes the child guilty
of original sin. What makes the child's experience parallel to
Adam's is that the sin he falls into after birth is worse than that
with which he was born:

> And that our Misery proceedeth ten thousand times more
> from the outward Bondage of Opinion and Custom, then
> from any inward corruption or Depravation of Nature: And
> that it is not our Parents Loyns, so much as our Parents lives,
> that Enthrals and Blinds us. Yet is all our Corruption De-
> rived from Adam: inasmuch as all the Evil Examples and
> inclinations of the World arise from His Sin.   (C, III, 8)[13]

Only when eternity-time's characteristics of simultaneity and
succession are confused can there be a problem in regard to
Traherne and the idea of pre-existence. On the line of time
there is a point at which each man is created; he does not exist
before that point. The particular time of this creation for Traherne is, I believe, that of conception in the womb:

> From Dust I rise,
> And out of Nothing now awake,
> These Brighter Regions which salute mine Eys,
> A Gift from GOD I take.
> The Earth, the Seas, the Light, the Day, the Skies,
> The Sun and Stars are mine; if those I prize.
>
> Long time before
> I in my Mothers Womb was born,
> A GOD preparing did this Glorious Store,
> The World for me adorne.
> ("The Salutation," 25-34)

Though he was "Nothing" throughout all the previous succession of eternity-time, his being is now established in that eternity subsequent to his creation. Since the whole line of time is
always existent in all of its parts, this human soul has, from a
different point of view, always existed; but then so has everything else.

From Innocence, man, in Adam, fell to Misery. This came
about through sin, both his own and that of another. In individual human lives it is the sins of ourselves and those we love that

briñg us to Misery, and even Christ was made a man of sorrows
through the sins which he took upon himself, although they
were not his own. Misery, however, is not a static condition, not
a resting place. It is always coupled with some measure of Grace
by which we are enabled to climb back up. These two
concurrent conditions form our estate of trial in this world
through which we work out our own salvation:

> For this purpose we are to remember, that our present Estate
> is not that of Reward, but Labour: It is an Estate of Trial,
> not of Fruition: A Condition wherein we are to Toyl, and
> Sweat, and travail hard, for the promised Wages; and Ap-
> pointed Seed Time, for a future Harvest; a real Warfare, in
> order to a Glorious Victory.   (CE, p. 19)

This upward struggle is an attempt to relearn man's own true
nature as the image of God. "Being vilely corrupted, you
have lost the sence of all these Realities, and are ignorant of the
Excellences of your own Estate and Nature" (CE, p. 37). Adam
and Eve had their trial too, which they failed; but with coming
of Grace in the form of Christ, man has been "restored to a *new
Estate of Trial*, and endued with Power to do new Duties, as
pleasing to him, as those which he required us in Eden" (CE, p.
105). Thus, as the Second Adam went through Misery and
by the Grace of God achieved Glory, so each of us go upward by
imitating Him:

> *O only begotten Son of God, Redeemer of the World, seeing
> thou didst Create and Redeem me that I might Obey and
> Imitate thee, make me to Obey and Imitate thee in all thy
> imitable Perfection.* ("Thanksgivings for the Body," 530-533)

This work is a mental, spiritual expansion of the soul's perception, the work which we saw begun by knowledge in the understanding. Traherne specifically applies the effect of Christ's
work to individual perception:

> My understanding . . . is like Jesus Christ, my Elder Brother,
> by whom it is Restored to its first power, and again Called to
> be a Son of God, by Him who Bringeth into His Eternal
> Glory.   ("Select Meditations," I, 91)

Christ's work of redemption made the estate of Glory possible, an estate like Innocence in many ways, as the Paradise which will come will be like Eden, but far superior to it. Glory is something experienced fully only after death, but we learn of it and prepare for it here on earth by means of our love for God. This love of God is the activity we have been treating throughout this study:

> It is to see and desire, to Esteem and delight in his Omnipresence and Eternity, and in every Thing by which he manifesteth himself in either of these, so that all Enlargement, and Greatness, and Light, and Perfection, and Beauty, and Pleasure, are founded in it, and to Love him to Perfection implies all Learning and Attainment, because we must necessarily be acquainted with all Things in all Worlds, before we can thorowly and compleatly do it. Which here upon Earth to do by Inclination and Endeavour to the utmost of our Power, is all that is required of us; And if we do it to our utmost, it shall be rewarded in the Beatifick Vision, with a full and Blessed Perfection, with an actual Love exactly resembling his, and fully answerable to it in the Highest Heavens. (*CE*, p. 140)

Knowledge is the means of foreseeing and eventually coming to Glory. Traherne sees knowledge as a stream which flows through all of the estates:

> The Original of our Knowledge is his Godhead, His Essence and his will are the Fountain of it; and the stream so excellent, that in all Estates it is for ever to be continued, as the Light and Glory of the whole Creation. . . . If we would *be perfect, as our Father which is in Heaven is perfect*, our Power of Knowing must be transformed (into *Act*,) and all Objects appear in the interior Light of our *own* understanding. . . . For not to *be*, and not to *appear*, are the same thing to the understanding. (*CE*, pp. 36-37)

Knowledge itself is not its own end. We learn and expand the mind's vision of eternity-time in order that we may eventually find our true nature as the image of God in all respects, may come to express all of the divine attributes:

> To be Partaker of the Divine nature, to be filled with all the

Fulness of GOD, to enter into his Kingdom and Glory, to be transformed into his Image, and made an Heir of GOD, and a joynt Heir with Christ, to live in Union and Communion with GOD, and to be made a Temple of the Holy Ghost; these are Divine and transcendent things that accompany our Souls in the Perfection of their Bliss and Happiness: the Hope and Belief of all which is justified, and made apparent by the explanation of the very nature of the Soul, its Inclinations and Capacities, the reality, and greatness of those Vertues of which we are capable, and all those objects which the Univers affordeth to our Contemplation.   (CE, p. 22)

And it is here finally that "Eternity in all its Beauties and Treasures," will be "seen, desired, esteemed, enjoyed" (CE, p. 35). "Where all Regions, and Ages, and Spaces, and Times, and Eternities, shall be before our Eys, and all Objects in all Worlds at once Visible, and infinitely Rich, and Beautiful, and *Ours!*" (CE, p. 123).

This will be the condition of the soul in Glory. The soul will not exist simply as a static reflection of the divine attributes but will fulfill its being by participation in action, specifically, according to Traherne, in the act of giving praise and thanks. For man's gratitude is the reflection of God's love: "Thus when I see my self infinitely beloved, I conceive a Gratitude as infinite in me" (CE, p. 265).

Here upon Earth there are disquiets, and desires, and expectations, and Complaints, and defects, and imperfections, fears and interests to be still secured, that lame and darken our Contentment and Gratitude. But in Heaven all these admixtures of alloy are remov'd. The glory of the light in which our Gratitude appeareth, adds lustre and beauty to the increase of its Perfection. In the utmost height of our Satisfaction there is such an infinite and eternal *force,* that our Gratitude breaks out in exulting and triumphing Effusions; all our Capacities, Inclinations, and Desires being fully satisfied, we have nothing else to do, but to Love and be Grateful.   (CE, p. 273)

If the resentment be wholly Spiritual, the Soul perhaps may be transformed to Gratitude, as Gratitude is to Contentment, and Praise, and Thanksgiving. But it will have no Body, no frail and corruptible Flesh, no bones or members to look after. All its operations are of one kind, all its works and concernments are the same.   (CE, p. 275)

Traherne's own "Thanksgivings" and those other sections of his work devoted solely to praise are his earthly attempt to fulfill the divine function of the soul. Like Augustine, Traherne sees David's Psalms as a type of what will come in the New Jerusalem. The Psalms were to Augustine symbols of the harmony and unity of the City. To Traherne they are like the praises of a soul which has been transformed into an act of gratitude. "O that I were as *David*, the sweet Singer of *Israel!* / In meeter Psalms to set forth thy praises. / Thy Raptures ravish me, and turn my soul all into melody" ("Thanksgivings for the Body," 341-343). But praise is not something confined to the soul anticipating Glory or actually existing in it. Of this world, also, Traherne asks, "Are not Praises the very End for which the World was created?" (*C*, III, 82). The Psalms of David exhibit this twofold nature of praise:

When I saw those Objects celebrated in His Psalmes which GOD and Nature had proposed to me, and which I thought chance only presented to my view: you cannot imagine how unspeakably I was delighted, to see so Glorious a Person, so Great a Prince, so Divine a Sage, that was a Man after Gods own Heart by the testimony of God Himself, rejoycing in the same things, meditating on the same and Praising GOD for the same. For by this I perceived we were led by one Spirit: and that following the clew of Nature into this Labyrinth I was brought into the midst of Celestial Joys: and that to be retired from Earthly Cares and fears and Distractions that we might in sweet and heavenly Peace contemplat all the Works of GOD, was to live in Heaven and the only way to becom what David was a Man after Gods own Heart.   (*C*, III, 70)

Traherne's view of thanksgiving is like that of Isaac Barrow. In his "Commonplace Book," Traherne copied extensively from Barrow's sermon, *On the Duty and Reward of Bounty to the Poor*.[14] But Barrow had earlier preached two sermons on "The Duty of Thanksgiving," sermons which show not only an attitude toward thanksgiving like Traherne's but also a marked similarity in temperament. Barrow says that thanksgiving

implies a right Apprehension of, and consequently a considerate Attention unto Benefits conferred. For he that is either wholly ignorant of his obligations, or mistakes them, or passes them over with a slight and superficial view, can no-wise

be gratefull. . . . This Duty requires a faithfull Retention of
Benefits in memory, and consequently frequent Reflexions
upon them.[15]

Barrow refers the reader to "that great pattern of Gratitude, the
Royal Prophet *David*" (p. 93). Thanksgiving for Barrow is
no mere state of passive gratitude for benefits received. "Yea, 'tis
our duty, not to be contented onely, but to be delighted, to
be transported, to be ravished with the emanations of his love"
(p. 96). The road of gratitude for Barrow, as for Traherne,
seems to lead to God himself,

> to be sensible of whose Beneficence, to meditate on whose
> Goodness, to admire whose Excellency, to celebrate whose
> Praise, is Heaven it self and Paradise, the life of Angels, the
> quintessence of joy, the supreme degree of Felicity. (p. 103)

Innocence, Misery, Grace, Glory: this, then, is the progress
which plays such an important part in Traherne's work. It is the
pattern of universal and individual history:

> By fall into sin I revolted from His Love & Defaced His
> Glory. Neither could I by any other means be Redeemed from
> Hell but by the Incarnation of His Son, by whose Death I
> am restored to Glory.   ("Select Meditations," II, 6)

It is also a pattern reflected in the structure of Traherne's
Centuries. The *Centuries* are about the journey of the soul
through these estates, teaching the reader how to expand his
thought to include all. They are also a personal exercise on the
part of their author in the use of this system of meditation.
Having shown in general terms what Traherne associated with
each of these estates, we can now deal with the structure of the
Centuries and with the function of eternity-time and of these
estates within that work.

NOTES

1. *The Lord of History*, trans. Nigel Abercrombie, p. 214.
2. See Patrick Fairburn, *The Typology of Scripture* (Edinburgh, 1854)
and also G. W. H. Lampe and K. J. Woolcombe, *Essays on Typology*
(Naperville, Illinois, 1957).

3. There are exceptions to Madsen's criteria in Keach; in William Guild, *Moses Unvailed* (London, 1620) ; and in Hermann Witsius, *De Oeconomia Foederum Dei Cum Hominibus*, (Leeuwarden, 1677) .

4. *The Authorised Version of the English Bible 1611*, ed. William Aldis Wright (Cambridge, 1909) , V [The New Testament]. Subsequent quotations are from this edition.

5. Irenaeus and the Adam-Christ typology is discussed by Jean Daniélou in *From Shadows to Reality*, trans. Dom Wulstan Hibberd, pp. 30-47.

6. W. D. Davies, *Paul and Rabbinic Judaism* (London, 1965) , p. 57.

7. *The Ante-Nicene Fathers*, trans. Alexander Roberts and James Donaldson, I, 456.

8. "The Eight Questions of Dulcitus" in *Saint Augustine: Treatises on Various Subjects*, trans. Sister Mary Sarah Muldowney *et al.* in *The Fathers of the Church*, ed. Roy Joseph Deferrari, XIV, 464. In addition Augustine also refers to Acts 13:21-23.

9. *The City of God*, trans. Marcus Dods, II, 199.

10. *Modern Philology*, XXXI (1934) , 274-275.

11. As I was writing this chapter, Arthur Leo Clements' *The Mystical Poetry of Thomas Traherne* was published (Cambridge, Mass., 1969) . Clements' title perhaps sufficiently indicates the difference in our respective points of view. Clements does, though, see a progressive development taking place in the poems of the Dobell MS., a progress which he sees as threepart, from innocence to redemption. Clements does not, except in one footnote, deal with this growth in terms of Traherne's estates.

12. "Seperat Souls" means souls separated from their bodies.

13. For a good defense of this interpretation of Traherne's view on original sin see George R. Guffey, "Thomas Traherne on Original Sin," *Notes & Queries*, XIV (1967) , 98-100.

14. See Carol L. Marks, "Thomas Traherne's Commonplace Book."

15. *The Works of the Learned Isaac Barrow, D. D.* (London, 1683) , p. 92.

V

The Journey Outward

Traherne's *Centuries* teach the soul by precept and example how to expand to "all things" and thus how to gain the perception and knowledge of everything in eternity and time. But this "all" is not something learned in a flash of insight. It is a process of learning with which Traherne was concerned, and learning is completed in parts; by degrees we come to truth. Within the *Centuries*, the "all" is divided for consideration into three main parts: "GOD, THE WORLD, YOUR SELF. *All Things* in Time and Eternity being the Objects of your Felicity GOD the Giver, and you the Receiver" (*C*, II, 100). In his structuring of the *Centuries*, Traherne treats these parts in an ascending order according to their importance. The world is the primary topic of Century I and of Century II through section 69; the individual soul, the topic of meditation from II, 70 through Century IV; and God is the subject of the Fifth Century.

The consideration of any one of these topics does not exclude the other two, just as the things themselves do not exclude each other. The direction of each of these main meditations, along with their purpose, remains consistent. The typological habit of thought discussed in the last chapter plays an important part throughout these meditations, and of special significance is the progressive development from the estate of Innocence through Misery and Grace to Glory, a development traced through once at length in both the discussion of the world and in that of the individual soul. In each case this journey is described in terms appropriate to the main subject under consideration. The broad line of movement of each of the three main sections and of the entire *Centuries* is one of advancement into the presence of God, where the individual, mirror-like soul participates in the

74

divine image in act as well as in potential, becomes omniscient and eternal.

Other readers of the *Centuries* have attempted to plot out an order for "what sometimes appears to be the chaotic disarray of Traherne's paragraphs."[1] Allan H. Gilbert, for one, deals with "The Structure of *Centuries of Meditations*" in his article, "Thomas Traherne as Artist," published in 1947 in *Modern Language Quarterly*. There he attempts to group the meditations according to their subject matter and according to their closeness to, or distance from, "conventional religion and normal theology" (p. 323). Gilbert's treatment is largely descriptive in nature, and his divisions somewhat arbitrarily chosen. Of the whole, he concludes:

> The effect is as though each one of the groups of kindred Meditations was written independently and the groups were then combined with little thought of their relation to each other, except perhaps as a matter of contrast or compensation. (p. 326)

In his edition of the *Centuries*, H. M. Margoliouth gives a descriptive account of the structure by means of the summaries which precede his notes on each Century. Here such things as his phrasing, the ideas he emphasizes, as well as the direct indication of groups, show those units which he feels belong together.

A general structural principle for the whole of the *Centuries* was proposed by Louis Martz in *The Paradise Within*. Martz treats the *Centuries* in terms of an Augustinian meditation and finds them "Augustinian, in theme, in style, in method of meditation" (p. 54). In an Augustinian meditation

> The mind in "cogitation" draws together, re-collects, the fragmentary hints of truth scattered about in the things that are made, and in this way moves toward an apprehension of the essential Idea that lives within the eternal mind of God. (pp. 47-48)

This is related to the Platonic notion of innate ideas, a belief Traherne did not hold, though this philosophical difference would not necessarily have precluded his use of a similar method of structuring thought in terms of external things. Martz sees the *Centuries* as particularly like Bonaventure's *Itinerarium Mentis in Deum*, which is Augustinian in method and is in part structured around a journey, the stages of which are those three used by Traherne:

> The first stage . . . consists in finding God by his traces in the external world; the second consists in finding God within the self, through discovering his image in man; and the third consists in contemplation of the essential attributes of God and the Trinity.   (p. 56)

Martz's account, however, differs from mine in that he does not see the First Century as part of this ternary structure but solely as a preparation, equivalent to the Prologue of Bonaventure's *Itinerarium*. In addition, Martz does not see the Fifth Century as the third stage of this development but as a state of "repose" which Bonaventure and Augustine placed "beyond the division of [the] basic threefold arrangement" (p. 57). Martz sees the entire Second Century as dealing with "the Creatures of the external world" (p. 57) and treats the Fourth Century rather than the Fifth as the last part of the three-fold journey. He thus sees this Fourth Century as concerned with God and his essence, while I, here, find it a consideration of man and the principles by which he should live and advance.

Joan Webber has said that, "Like other Anglican works, the *Centuries* reflect different aspects of themselves to different readers, or even to the same reader."[2] The present account of the *Centuries* differs from accounts of a purely descriptive nature. Specific ideas and groupings, while identified, are seen working together in a more important whole, a whole with a definite pattern and direction. If this differs from Martz, it is because I am here treating the *Centuries* according to a method of meditation that Traherne himself has outlined in his other works as well as in the *Centuries*, a method based upon his all-inclusive estates and his philosophy of the relationship of man and eternity-time. By not attempting to find parallels for all the parts of someone else's book or system, and by not believing that Traherne goes beyond the bounds of human knowledge as he saw them to an ultimate "repose" in those empty pages after the Fifth Century, I find the three-part division of being (the world, man and God) sufficient for the major structure of Traherne's work. Whatever the sources of this division (and perhaps it was too much of a commonplace in the Renaissance to attribute to Augustine with any great degree of relevance), my own concern is more with how, according to Traherne, the soul or mind, by knowledge and love, may come to know all things in all three of these areas of what exists.

The beginning of the First Century makes plain the purpose of the whole work.

> An Empty Book is like an Infants Soul, in which any Thing may be Written. It is Capable of all Things, but containeth Nothing. I hav a Mind to fill this with Profitable Wonders.   (1)

The analogy between the growth of knowledge in the soul and what Traherne will do in this work is not a fortuitous one. This organic growth is as much a part of his method as it is of his philosophy.

Traherne goes on to say that he will speak of "those Truths you Love, without Knowing them" (1). Readers have asked how the very religious Mrs. Hopton, to whom the *Centuries* are addressed, could be said not to know these truths. But Traherne is not attributing ignorance to his friend; or at least if it is ignorance, he himself shares in it. There is "in us a World of Lov to somewhat, tho we know not what in the World that should be" (2). This "Great Thing" which is unknown, Traherne goes on to explain, is "that you should be Heir of the World" (3). Your true relationship, your "Fellowship" with the world, has always been; but it has become, even for Traherne, hidden in its full aspect. The total vision of all things, as we have seen already, is impossible in this mortal life. What is possible is an improved vision achieved through study and meditation. Such an improved vision gives an insight into the nature of this unknown relationship of man to the world and gives a promise of what the soul will be in Glory.

The path to a fuller vision of the world and of man's relationship to it is the subject of the First Century and the first sixty-nine sections of the Second Century. "It is my Design therefore in such a Plain maner to unfold it, that my Friendship may appear, in making you Possessor of the Whole World" (3). The path is not one of contention and argument; but "I after [God's] Similitide will lead you into Paths Plain and Familiar" where nothing will appear but "Contentment and

Thanksgiving" (4). The end of the journey toward God is not simply salvation; more importantly, it is "A Communion with Him in all His Glory" (5). Though salvation is wonderful, this communion, says Traherne, is really the end for which Jesus suffered. Such communion begins by means of the world, God's gift of love communicated to us as its rightful heirs.

The First Century gives the basic reasons for making a mental quest in search of the whole world (7-13), demonstrates the accessibility of such knowledge (14-24), and indicates by what signs you will know you have attained it (25-39). The remainder of the Century is a meditation on "wants," on the necessity of the world's being and of its being as it is. Within the meditation and culminating it (52-100) is a meditation on the most necessary thing in the world, love, that one thing which fulfills all wants. With the demonstrations of the First Century as its groundwork, the Second Century (through 69) is a meditation on the whole world in terms of Traherne's estates.

Let us return now to the First Century and follow this development more closely. In section 6 Traherne explains that his gift of the world is an act of love by which his friend may be "Advanced to the Throne of God, and may see His Lov." The end of this section forms a transition to that group giving reasons for seeking such an advancement. The gift of the world "will enable you also, to contemn the World, and to overflow with Praises." In explaining this, Traherne makes the important distinction that there are two worlds, that which God created and that of man. The world Traherne is giving through his meditations is that of God, and you must "Leav the one that you may enjoy to other" (7). That the method of doing so is meditation, Traherne makes clear in the following three sections. "What is more Easy and Sweet then Meditation? yet in this hath God commended his Lov, that by Meditation it is Enjoyed" (8). "Is it not Easy to conceiv the World in your mind?" (9). But merely thinking of the world is not enough; knowledge of its "Use and Value" must be constantly retained in mind. Note that here again it is value and process that is more important for Traherne than things themselves. To think well is not simply to hold material things in mind.

To think well is to serv God in the Interior Court: To hav a Mind composed of Divine Thoughts, and set in frame, to be

Like Him within. To Conceiv aright and to Enjoy the
World, is to Conceiv the Holy Ghost, and to see His Lov;
Which is the Mind of the Father.   (10)

Such meditation, the remaining sections of this group (11-13)
continue, makes the soul holy by making it the image of God.

For then we Pleas God when we are most like Him. we
are like Him when our Minds are in Frame. our Minds are
in Frame when our Thoughts are like his. And our Thoughts
are then like his when we hav such Conceptions of all
objects as God hath, and Prize all Things according to their
value.   (13)

Having stated the purpose of meditation on the world, to
"conceiv the World in your Mind" as God does in his, Traherne
is aware of the immediate problem this brings up: how can
the whole world be said to be accessible to any one man? The
following sections (14-24) attempt to answer this unstated question. Traherne demonstrates the accessibility of the whole world
to one man on the bases of the nature of creation, the nature
of God, and the nature of the human soul.

Rightly seen, every thing has a "Proper Place" in the
creation, "serves us in its Place" (14), and has its use and value
only when in its proper relationship to the world and man. The
creation of Adam, without companions at first, was meant to
indicate typologically that all things in the world were made for
the individual man as well as for all men (14);[3] the
creation of other men increased the number of things available
to any one man, "Angels and Men being all mine" (15). God in
his nature of father and benefactor has given the whole
world to us as a gift (16). Traherne goes on to speak of the
nature of this gift. "The WORLD," he reminds the reader, "is not
this little Cottage of Heaven and Earth. Tho this be fair, it is
too small a Gift" (18); it is not compatible with the nature of
God. The world includes "the Heavens and the Heavens of
Heavens, and the Angels and the Celestial Powers" (18). The
world includes not only what exists in eternity-time but all
things in the eternity outside of time as well, "all those infinit
and Eternal Treasures that are to abide for ever, after the Day
of Judgment" (18).

Traherne concludes his demonstration of the availability of
the whole world with a discussion of the nature of man and his
soul in their relationship to the world (19-24). The soul is
greater than the world and can easily encompass it.

> Alass the WORLD is but a little Centre in Comparison of
> you. . . . Your Understanding comprehends the World like
> the Dust of a Ballance, measures Heaven with a Span and
> esteems a thousand yeers but as one Day. So that Great
> Endless Eternal Delights are only fit to be its Enjoyments.
> (19)

Besides the God-like nature of the understanding, the divine
laws under which man is governed have made the world accessible because, in requiring us to love God, they require us to
love His works. Seeing the world as the work of God makes it
"the Beautifull Frontispiece of Eternitie. the Temple of God"
(20). Divine law also established the world as something to
serve us, and the consequent love of creation for us makes our
love of all creation possible.

Man's senses, furthermore, make the world available to him.
Though they cannot perceive everything at once, their use in
the correct enjoyment of seen things will lead eventually to
those things which are as yet unseen:

> Prize these first: and you shall Enjoy the Residue. Glory,
> Dominion, Power, Wisdom, Honor, Angels, Souls, Kingdoms,
> Ages. *Be faithfull in a little, and you shall be Master over
> much.*   (21)

Even the inclinations of the soul (its desires) prove the world
ours. Covetousness and ambition as they usually appear in the
world of man are simply misdirections of noble inclinations
which, if rightly directed, would enable us to possess everything
(22-24). The world, then, is naturally available to the knowledge of man; it is a knowledge which readily becomes love as
the nature of its object is clearly seen.

With the availability of the whole world to an individual man
now established, the next question Traherne chooses to answer might be put this way: Since it is possible for me to know
the world and thus love it, how will I know when my vision is

correct? How, in other words, will I know I have succeeded?
Traherne treats the signs of success (as well as the marks of the
unsuccessful) from section 25 through 39. In his description of
what it is to know the world correctly, Traherne has created
some of the most beautiful prose of the *Centuries*.

> Your Enjoyment of the World is never right, till you so Es-
> teem it, that evry thing in it, is more your Treasure, then a
> Kings Exchequer full of Gold and Silver. . . . I remember the
> Time, when the Dust of the Streets were as precious as Gold
> to my Infant Eys, and now they are more precious to the Ey
> of Reason.   (25)

> You never Enjoy the World aright, till you see how a Sand
> Exhibiteth the Wisdom and Power of God: And Prize in evry
> Thing the Service which they do you, by Manifesting His
> Glory and Goodness to your Soul.   (27)

> Your Enjoyment of the World is never right, till evry Morn-
> ing you awake in Heaven: see your self in your fathers Pal-
> ace: and look upon the Skies and the Earth and the Air, as
> the Celestial Joys: having such a Reverend Esteem of all, as if
> you were among the Angels.   (28)

Yet some men despise God's works and world for their own and
thus lose everything. In the presence of glories, they will not
open their eyes; thus "the World is both a Paradice and a Prison
to different Persons" (36). Loving all things rightly, Traherne sums up, makes us to *"live in His Image. and to do so, is
to live in Heaven"* (39).

With the accessibility of the whole world and the signs that
one is esteeming it correctly now set forth, Traherne begins a
meditation on the world as an infinite gift that was infinitely
necessary, a meditation on "wants" (40-100). In treating God's
gifts, this meditation is unavoidably involved in the treatment
of Grace; for the greatest and most necessary gift was, of course,
Jesus Christ in His work of Redemption. The First Century
climaxes in a meditation on the cross; and this meditation is in
line with what Traherne had said about Christ's purpose in the
world at the beginning of this Century: the cross is a sign of
God's gift of communion with Him through love. But since this
Century is about the world rather than about God directly, most
of this meditation on the cross deals with the communion

of love as it occurs among men in the world, Christ's gift of love
being the prime example for our love of others.

The world consists of wants and supplies, of necessities and
that which meets those necessities. Every want must have its
supply or God's creation would not be perfect. As a picture must
be made up of areas of light and areas of shadow, says
Traherne, so our fulfillment, our "Felicitie," requires the recognition of wants and supplies (41). This dual nature exists in us,
in the world, and in the relationship of man to the world, for
we were made to want everything. "He made us to Want like
GODS, that like GODS we might be satisfied" (41). God himself
"from all Eternity Wanted like a GOD" (41). We can accept that
God is supplied with all things possible, that all things are
before him; and since we are His image, we can see the possibility of this becoming true for us. But how, then, can God, who
never fell, be said to want what he always has? Traherne finds
an answer for this question in the nature of eternity and time:

> He is infinitly Glorious, becaus all His Wants and Supplies
> are at the same time in his Nature from Eternity. He had,
> and from Eternity He was without all His Treasures.
> From Eternity He needed them, and from Eternity He en-
> joyed them. For all Eternity is at once in Him. both
> the Empty Durations before the World was made, and the
> full ones after. His Wants are as Lively as His Enjoy-
> ments: And always present with Him. For His Life is Per-
> fect, and He feels them both.   (44)

The only way to understand a passage like this is to see the
world in terms of eternity-time, an infinite succession permanent in all its parts. Wants come before their supplies in the
succession of eternity-time, since they were in being before the
world was created. But from the point of view of eternity, seeing
the infinite, eternal extension as a whole, all wants and all
supplies have always been.

It is not enough to perceive the world in your mind or soul.
Value is more important than being. You must see how everything in the world meets a particular need. In that eternity
before your creation, though temporally non-existent, you were
eternally in need of being; indeed, you were in need of everything.

What you wanted from all Eternity, be sensible of to all
Eternity. Let your Wants be present from Everlasting.
Is not this a Strange Life to which I call you? Wher-
in you are to be present with Things that were before the
World was made? And at once present even like GOD with
infinit Wants and infinit Treasures: Be present with your
Want of a Diety, and you shall be present with the Dietie.
(45)

Though neither we nor the world existed before that point in
eternity-time when we were created, we can see into the eternity
before the creation by knowing our wants.

Sections 46-50 contain those remarks by Traherne on the
nature of hell which some readers have found uncharacteristic
and unpleasant. Traherne says that men who do not esteem
their blessings, their wants and supplies, while here on earth
where they have them shall see them throughout eternity, from
hell, where they will not have them. And hell, says Traherne,
"is fitly mentioned in the Enjoyment of the World: And is it
self by the Happy Enjoyed, as a Part of the world" (48). Of
course, everything in creation is to be enjoyed by the happy,
who see all things working together for good; but this mental
hell of Traherne's has a rather permanent nature to it which
makes it something a little different from the vicissitudes of
earthly life. The only justification I would offer is that this is a
logical result of Traherne's philosophy of human development.
The progress from Innocence to Glory that takes place in history and in individual lives is an organic one; if one refuses to
participate and does not grow toward his divine nature as the
image of God, how may he in the moment at which he should be
admitted to Glory suddenly make up for the time and the
growth he has lost? Since no part of the succession of time can
ever be erased, the result seems inevitable and, though perhaps
not kind, at least natural. If one refuses to grow, he may not
expect to be part of the harvest.

The subject now becomes man's wants as a means of communion. Joan Webber has treated communion in Traherne in her
book, *The Eloquent "I,"* where she sees it as informing the
purpose of the entire *Centuries.* In this last part of the First
Century, the sort of communion primarily treated appears to be
that between man and other men in the world, an image of the
communion between man and God and a reflection of the

communion of love between the perfect man, Christ, and those He came to redeem.

But before dealing directly with love among men in the world, Traherne draws the divine pattern. It is because of our communion with God, says Traherne, that our lives and the whole world are ours; for "In Him you feel, in Him you liv, and mov and hav your Being. in Him you are Blessed. Whatsoever therfore serveth Him serveth you and in Him you inherit all Things" (52). When you correctly will the presence of God's world into your mind, you are communing with God in the very act of creation (53), an act which is more important than its results. Though Traherne talks of God and man in these sections, he always speaks of them in terms of his main subject, knowing the world.

When one is "all; Or in all, and with all" (53), all particular things within eternity are known to him:

All the Joys and all the Treasures, all the Counsels and all the Perfections all the Angels and all the Saints of GOD are with Him. All the Kingdoms of the World and the Glory of them are continualy in his Ey: The Patriarchs Prophets and Apostles are always before Him. The Counsels and the fathers, the Bishops and the Doctors minister unto Him. All Temples are Open before Him, The Melodie of all Quires reviveth Him, the Learning of all Universities doth employ him, the Riches of all Palaces Delight him, The Joys of Eden Ravish Him, The Revelations of S. John Transport Him, The Creation and the Day of Judgment pleas Him, The Hosannas of the Church Militant, and the Hallelujahs of the Saints Triumphant fill Him, The Splendor of all Coronations entertain Him, the Joys of Heaven surround Him, / And our Saviors Cross like the Centre of Eternity is in Him, It taketh up his Thoughts, and exerciseth all the Powers of his soul, with Wonder Admiration Joy and Thanksgiving. The Omnipotence of God is His Hous, and Eternity his Habitation.   (54)

Throughout this Century recognition of the importance of man's knowledge and vision of eternity has been growing. The purpose of the soul's expansion to the omniscience and all-lovingness of God is for Traherne not so much that it may be present with the world in the current moment of time and space, but that it may be present with all creation at all times and, especially, that it may be present with the important events of our history. Of all those events, Christ's gift from the cross is the most important. In the following sections, dealing with the cross, Traherne illustrates that power of the soul in regard to the world which he has described in the passage just quoted above. Although it is at times not considered directly, the center of eternity, the cross, is the vantage point from which the remaining sections of the Century (55-100) are written.

"The Contemplation of Eternity maketh the Soul Immortal" begins section 55. Such contemplation is not of a memory or a recollection of forgotten things hidden in the soul of man; the soul can actually

> see before and after its Existence into Endless Spaces. Its Sight is its Presence. And therfore is the Presence of the understanding endless, because its Sight is so. O what Glorious Creatures should we be, could we be present in Spirit with all Eternity!   (55)

Traherne then traces Biblical history, speaking of the soul's power to be present in Eden, present with Enoch and Moses, in Aaron's tabernacle and in Canaan, and present with Solomon. "But abov all these our Saviors Cross is the Throne of Delights. That Centre of Eternity, That Tree of Life in the midst of the Paradice of GOD!" (55).

"There are we Entertained with the Wonder of all Ages. There we enter into the Heart of the Univers" (56). It is because of Christ's demonstration of the communion between God and man that we are able to see all things in eternity and time with our souls, that we are able to become in a more glorious way the image of God in which we were originally created.

> When I am lifted up saith the Son of man I will draw all Men unto me. . . . so shall we be Drawn by that Sight from Ignorance and Sin and Earthly vanities, idle sports Companions Feasts and Pleasures, to the Joyful Contemplation of that Eternal Object. But by what Cords? The Cords of a Man, and the Cords of Lov.   (56)

The cross is the "Gate of Heaven" (58), the symbol of the grace

by which we are able to perceive our Glory, our existence in the
nature of God, while here on earth and, after death, participate
in it. It is that place from which we may see eternity (59). It is
the burning tree "In the light of which we see how to possess all
the Things in Heaven and Earth after His Similitud" (60).
We learn many things from the cross, but most importantly "we
learn to imitat Jesus in his Lov unto all" (61). Martz has noted
the shift in the position of the cross from "there" to "here" in
this section (p. 64). We can see this shift as an indication of
the continuing growth of the soul's vision of, and presence with,
things in eternity-time.

What follows is a prayer to Christ desiring to be more like
Him, especially in His love toward man in giving His gift, a gift
which enables us to be aware of how all our wants are met
(knowledge requisite, we recall, for entrance into Glory). Traherne desires to see better how he is loved in order that he
might love others better (63). The proofs of God's love to him
are the gift of the world (64-65); of more importance, the gift
of his body (66); and, greatest of all, the gift of a soul in God's
image (67). Seeing these things, through the Grace of Christ, he
is able to love all men in the world better, to see how much
more glorious the world is because of the creation of other men.
The love that circulates between God and man, this "communion," is reproduced in the love between a man and men. "In
evry Soul whom Thou hast Created, Thou hast given me the
Similitude of thy self, to Enjoy!" (69). The laws of God
require that you love as He does. To meet this requirement you
were given "a Comprehension infinit to see all Ages" (72). "Yea
by Loving Thou Expandest and Enlargest thy self" (73).

Throughout, Traherne has occasionally placed himself the-
oretically "in Adams steed" (65) or used the pronoun "I" to
mean man in general. (Joan Webber furnishes a thorough discussion of Traherne's use of this pronoun.) It is in both man-
ners that this "I" is used in section 75:

> Being to lead this Life within I was placed in Paradice
> without with som Advantages which the Angels hav not.
> And being Designed to Immortality and an Endless Life, was
> to Abide with GOD from everlasting to everlasting in all His
> Ways. But I was Deceived by my Appetite, and fell into
> Sin. Ingratefully I despised Him that gave me my Being.

I offended in an Apple against Him that gave me the whole
World: But Thou O Savior art here upon the Cross suffering
for my Sins. What shall I render unto Thee for so Great a
Mercy!

But the "I" still remains the individual Traherne enabled
through Grace to see these things, a perception which is also,
because of the communion of love, a participation. Traherne
says that it is because of the gift of Christ's love that man is
again able to enjoy the world, though now in an even better way
than Adam could (76). Traherne himself has not come to
the total vision of Glory, but he longs for it and will come to it
through love of those other men who are in this world (78-79).
    None of this Century has been digressive. Traherne's method
of treating the possession of the world by the soul has been one
of a logical, organic development of his case. Topics have been
treated in their order of importance. These topics were the
world's accessibility, the signs of possession, and the nature of
the world as want and supply. The main grouping, the last, has
developed from a general consideration of wants and supplies to
a treatment of the very greatest necessity, love, primarily
(for the subject of this Century is the world) the love of others.
Traherne now turns again to address directly the "Excellent
friend" for whom the Centuries were written. The transition is
a natural one. The prayer to love others better and to "make all
them that are round about me Wise and Holy as Thou art"
(79) is part of a natural progression which began with the
treatment of the love of God to man and becomes more and
more specific in its application of this love to human relationships until Traherne turns to his friend.
    Traherne and his friend, again because of the blood of Christ,
are united in communion and can "see and Lov and Enjoy
each other at 100 Miles Distance" (80). He tells her that man is
incapable of directing any goodness toward God; goodness
should rather be turned toward His "Saints," "the Excellent in
the Earth in whom is all my Delight. To Delight in the Saints
of God is the Way to Heaven" (81). These saints are not just
those who live in goodness today, but "All the Saints of all Ages
and all Kingdoms" (81). There are, however, certain saints, most
worthy of love, who are living today but are perhaps the
hardest of all to discover because of the general corruption of

the rest of mankind (82). Yet, they must be sought out. Though
they will have human infirmities, they will still be able to
"Exchange Souls with you. . . . And half a Dozen such as these
wisely chosen will represent unto us the New Jerusalem" (83).
Participation in such a group of communicants allows each
member to see the Saviour (and all that this means) with the
eyes of all participants. This communion with others through
Christ

> will Enlarge your Soul and make you to Dwell in all King-
> doms and Ages. . . . By seeing the Saints of all Ages we are
> present with them. By being present with them becom
> too Great for our own Age, and near to our Savior.   (85)

Sections 86-98 are again addressed directly to the Saviour in
thanksgiving for the communion of love which enables a man to
be present in others and to enjoy Christ's Glory (86). Again
Traherne prays for greater ability:

> Remov the vail of thy flesh and I may see thy Glory. . . . let us
> see thy Understanding with our Understandings, and
> read thy Lov with our own. Let our Souls hav Com-
> munion with thy Soul, and let the Ey of our Mind enter
> into thine.   (88)

Section 89 is an awful vision of Christ's suffering on the cross, a
horrifying experience which can yet be enjoyed by us because
we ourselves can go through this experience for others in our
ascent to Glory (90). Traherne asks for the spirit of Christ that
it might bring him to eternity.

> O the Glory of that Endless Life, that can at once extend to
> all Eternity! Had the Cross been 20 Millions of Ages fur-
> ther, it had still been equaly near, nor is it possible to remov
> it, for it is with all Distances in my Understanding, and tho
> it be removed many thousand Millions of Ages more is as
> clearly seen and Apprehended. This Soul for which Thou
> diedst, I desire to Know more perfectly, O my Savior.   (92)

Traherne desires that his soul be in act what it is in potential.
The way is through "Union and Communion" (96). It is possible because of Christ's act of love.

The final two sections of the First Century sum up the message of the whole: the soul can know and love the whole world.

> He made us the sons of GOD in Capacity by giving us a Power, to see Eternity, to Survey His Treasures, to love his children, to know and to lov as He doth, to becom Righteous and Holy as He is; that we might be Blessed and Glorious as He is. . . . When we prize all the Things in Heaven and Earth, as He Prizeth Him, and make a Conscience of doing it as He doth after His similitude; then are we actually present with them, and Blessed in them.   (99)

The First Century began by comparing the soul of a child to an empty book; it ends, in section 100 (quoted in full in Chapter III, above), with a description of how objects, saints, ages and Christ, come into the soul.

> And the Kingdom of God (as our Savior saith, this Way) is within you; let us ever think and Meditat on Him, that His conception Nativity Life and Death may be always within us. Let Heaven and Earth Men and Angels, God and his Creatures be always within us.   (100)

The Second Century, through 69, is a meditation on the world in terms of Traherne's estates. It logically follows what we have just seen developing in the First Century. While that Century was concerned primarily with demonstrating the possibility of knowing and loving all things in the world, Traherne's Second Century begins by saying it will now give "Directions how to enjoy [the world]" (2). These directions are an exercise in that power treated in the previous Century, an exercise that is designed to expand the soul progressively to a vision of the world in eternity and time. This exercise works by means of a simultaneous application of the universal and individual meanings of each of Traherne's four estates. The remarkable consistency of this simultaneous vision, both here and elsewhere in Traherne's work, seems to be a direct result of his concept of eternity-time, a concept which, we recall, maintains the actual presence and interrelatedness of all things pertinent to universal and particular being.

After summing up "The Services which the World doth you" (1), Traherne begins his directions for meditation upon these

services, upon the use and value of the world; and these directions are themselves an exercise in the sort of meditation they
describe. The first step, says Traherne, is to place yourself
mentally in the estate of Innocence, and this estate is the subject
of section 2 through section 27. In this estate you must, in
effect, imitate Adam. You do not become Adam; but rather, you
participate in his experience, "commune" with the events of
his condition. "Place yourself in [the world] as if no one
were Created besides your self. And consider all the services it
doth, even to you alone" (2). The world is "the Beginning of
Gifts" (2) and the birthright of every child that comes into it.
Thus we see Adam, childhood, and the mind as it sees its
original condition, all working together as one in this part of the
Second Century.

Though Grace was first necessary that we might see Innocence (as was explained in the First Century), the dependency
is reciprocal. "Till you see that the World is yours, you cannot
weigh the Greatness of Sin, nor the Misery of your fall, nor
Prize your Redeemers Lov" (3). True understanding comes
about from an organic growth through the estates. Innocence
must be fully understood before Misery because "The Misery of
your fall . . . cannot be seen, till the Glory of the Estate
from which we are faln is Discerned" (4). And this is what our
Saviour meant when He counseled, *"Remember from whence
thou art faln, and Repent*. Which intimates our Duty of Remembering our Happiness in the Estate of Innocence" (5).
Knowing the world made for you, who are the Adam-man, and
knowing yourself made, like Adam, in God's image confirms
your faith in the Redemption (6).

Martz remarks that, in his discussion of the cross in the First
Century, Traherne says of Christ's wounds, "These Bloody Characters are too Dim to let me read [the Glory of thy Soul]" (I,
64) and then, because of this incapacity, "turns away from the
Cross to consider the Creation" (p. 64). What Traherne means
in this turning away is that we see Christ's Glory more through
His gift than through His body. The dual dependency of the
estates of Innocence and Grace discussed in the Second Century
also accounts for any apparent incompleteness in the treatment
of Grace in the First Century. The Second Century supplies
what was lacking.

Innocence, then, is the necessary starting point; and, with this established, Traherne says again, "Place yourself therfore in the midst of the World as if you were alone: and Meditat upon all the Services which it doth unto you" (7). What follows now is a consideration of the sun, first as if it were absent, then as it really is, in the necessity, wisdom and perfection of its creation to serve you (7-11). Although Traherne, his method demonstrated, decides to "say less of the rest" of creation (12), he notes that the air, the earth, the sea and all things in them were created in the same perfection and to the same end. "Why should you not render Thanks to God for them all? You are the Adam, or the Eve that Enjoy them" (12). Time in this meditation has been from the first the eternal "now." The world serves you, Adam, alone and it serves all men everywhere in time, if they would but see this.

In addition to those immediate and visible elements of the world whose services Traherne has just considered, there are also "Sublime and Celestial Services which the World doth do" (17); and thus through contemplation of the visible world we are led to the invisible one. God himself (the pattern for invisible as well as visible things) is necessarily invisible in order that all other possible things might have being (19). The only sort of body He might assume is that of the whole world (20). Indeed, "This visible World is the Body of GOD" (21); though, to be sure, it is a body He has taken on, not His natural form. Traherne does not draw the analogy, but it would seem that the presence of God in the world is a concept like that of the Incarnation of Christ. For most men of Traherne's period, it was a paradox and a "mystery" that the infinite and omnipresent God had taken on a body. The event of the Incarnation was seen as eternity bending down and, for a short period, touching time. For Traherne there was no paradox. The Incarnation is a reflection of the eternal fact of God's being. God is always in the world, and time is always in eternity. Because He has taken this world as His body, it is possible to come to the knowledge of the invisible, knowledge of things of the spirit, through a study of the perfections of the visible world. Like God, the world is infinite in being round (Whether space is infinite "we cannot tell" [21].) It has seemed to some to be eternal; and it expresses God's attributes of beauty, wisdom, goodness, and power.

But recall now that for Traherne, God and the things of the

spirit, of eternity-time, consist of "act," of motion and operation
rather than of matter. The visible world, then, could never have
been equated in value with God by Traherne, who says that
we may see God's power operating in the world. "How shall His
Life appear in that which is Dead?" Traherne asks for us
(22). The answer is, through motion. "Life is the Root of
Activity and Motion. . . . Motion being a far greater Evidence of
Life, then all Lineaments whatsoever" (22). When Traherne asks us to contemplate the created world as Adam saw it,
he is not particularly asking us to contemplate "things" such as a
flower, a tree, or even the sun. What we are to meditate
upon are the services, the operations, the processes, the invisible
qualities that are part of the nature of the object yet produce an
effect outside of that object. Not nature herself but the
actions of nature are that which is worthy of our knowledge and
love, "Beasts Fowls and Fishes teaching and evidencing the
Glory of their Creator. . . . All which are subservient unto Man"
(22).

   As with the rest of creation, the invisible things that are part
of the nature of man evidence God. As he was created the last
but most important of all the creation, so he is treated by
Traherne here (though elsewhere Traherne disagreed with the
Bible's account of the order of creation). Man has yet what was
given to him at his creation,

   a Dominion over all the rest and GOD over Him. . . . Man is
   made in the Image of GOD, and therfore is a Mirror and
   Representativ of Him. And Therfore in Himself He may
   see GOD, which is His Glory and Felicitie. His Thoughts
   and Desires can run out to Everlasting, His Lov can extend to
   all Objects, His Understanding is an endless Light, and can
   infinitely be present in all Places, and see and Examine all
   Beings, survey the reasons, surmount the Greatness, exceed
   the Strength, contemplat the Beauty, Enjoy the Benefit, and
   reign over all it sees and Enjoys like the Eternal GODhead.
   (23)

By contemplating the whole world you are not only able to
know God better, but you gain a better understanding of yourself as well (26). The "Prospect even of this World," then, is "a
Gate" through which we can "see into GODS Kingdom" (27),
that kingdom made up of man, God and the created world.

In seeing the nature of the love of God evident in the creation, we can also see "the Nature of all Righteousness opened and unfolded: with the Ground and foundations of Rewards and Punishments" (27). Traherne is not one to dwell long on unpleasant subjects; and his treatment of the loss of God's world (i.e., man's fall) and its subsequent estate of Misery lasts through only four sections (28-31). It is man's duty, Traherne says, to esteem the world correctly, "Which to do, is certainly the most Blessed Thing in all Worlds, as not to do it is most Wicked and most Miserable" (28). God is so righteous and this duty so blessed that "GOD cannot therfore but be infinitly provoked, when we break His Laws" (29). It is a mighty sin to despise the world, a sin of infinite proportion. "Yea one Act only of Despite done to the smallest Creature made you infinitly deformed. . . . Verily you are in Danger of Perishing Eternaly" (30). Each man sins as Adam did in misvaluing something in the creation; but God in his infinite wisdom knows a way "wherby to Sever the Sin from the Sinner. . . . And thus we com again by the Works of God to our Lord JESUS CHRIST" (31). We come again to the estate of Grace.

As in his treatment of the sun at the first of this Century, Traherne treats the perfect nature of his subject, how the appearance of Grace in the world could not possibly have come about in any better manner. No angel would have been more suitable than Christ for the task, since an angel is a creature and man can only be saved through the eternal Godhead (37). Thus mankind in general and we in particular can be saved through Christ, the Son (38). But, to re-emphasize, salvation is something more than release from sin. It is the renewal of divine communion. The following sections, like the discussion of Grace in the First Century, treat the communion of love. Love is like the Trinity. Indeed, it is God and has a threefold aspect. "In all Lov there is a Lov begetting, a Lov begotten, and a Lov Proceeding" (40). God begets love; His Son is that begotten love, and through Him we may receive it as the Holy Ghost. Though in three parts, it is an unbroken stream of love, a stream whose waters are eternally present all along its course and of equal purity and value everywhere. "Love in the Fountain, and Lov in the Stream are both the same. And therfore are they both Equal in Time and Glory. For Lov communicateth it self" (41). But this love is a stream which flows perpetually back upon itself, for it is "the Means also by which we see and Lov the Father" through Christ (44).

What follows (45-69) pertains to the estate of Glory, though necessarily a Glory seen from the estate of Grace. The subject is still love, but it is treated in a somewhat different way. The opening of section 45 indicates the nature of that difference.

How Wonderfull is it, that GOD by being Lov should prepare a Redeemer to Die for us? But how much more Wonderfull, that by this means Himself should be: and be GOD by being LOV!   (45)

Perhaps because of the length of its treatment in the First Century, love as it appears in the estate of Grace, typified by the love of Christ, has been treated only briefly; and the discussion now turns to "Love in the Fountain." Love in the estate of Innocence is primarily love for the created world as if you were created alone in it; love in the estate of Grace is an added love for your fellow men. Love in the estate of Glory is love for and from God when he is known directly; it is the love existent in all objects both created and increate, love of the world from the widest and clearest point of view.

And by being Lov GOD is the fountain of all Worlds. To receiv all and to be the End of all is Equally Delightfull, and by Being Lov GOD receiveth, and is the End of all. For all the Benefits that are don unto all, by Loving all, Himself receiveth.   (46)

God, Love, is His own end. The communion of love between God and the world is the means by which God has His being as Love. Love communicated is God as Act. The same is just as true for God's image, the human soul.

By loving a Soul does Propagat and beget it self. By loving it does Dilate and Magnify it self. By loving it does Enlarge and Delight it self. By Loving also it Delighteth others, as by Loving it doth Honor and Enrich it self. But above all by Loving it does attain itself. Lov also being the End of Souls, Which are never Perfect, till they are in Act, what they are in Power. . . . Till we becom therefore all Act as GOD is, we can never rest, nor ever be satisfied.   (48)

This is the reason we must know and love the world. Through love we are not only able to see but also to exist sensibly in all parts of eternity and thus of time. We are, through this communion of love, especially able to exist in other souls and be "The Brother of Christ Jesus, and One Spirit with the Holy Ghost" (50).

Adam, too, wanted to be like God; but he went about it in the wrong way, and thus "He lost all" (52). The correct way to be like God is "by Loving all as He doth" (52). When we come to love God directly, we shall not only reflect Him but be in actual communion with Him, experience things through Him. (It should be repeated here that one does not become God through this communion, any more than Christ could be said to become us when we partake of the Eucharist.) Though the two processes of reflection and communion can be discussed in separation, they are both necessary to each other in the completion of our enjoyment of the world. By these methods we are enabled to live in all; by living in all we live in God. "The more we liv in all the more we liv in one" (61).

Sections 62-69 conclude and climax the progressive development that has been taking place. The love of all, the communion of the soul with everything, is the end toward which all this has been directed; it is a vision of Glory in the world.

Lov is the true Means by which the World is Enjoyed. Our Lov to others, and Others Lov to us. . . . Love is the Soul of Life and Crown of Rewards. If we cannot be satisfied in the Natur of Lov we can never be satisfied at all. The very End for which GOD made the World was that He might Manifest His Lov.   (62)

"You are as Prone to lov, as the Sun is to shine. It being the most Delightfull and Natural Employment of the Soul of man" (65). Love for one person is "but a little spark" of true love (66). We must beware of loving any one thing too much. We can never come right until we love all things and love them in their true relationship to us. "What a World would this be, were evry thing Beloved as it ought to be!" (67).

Traherne concludes this progress with another direct address to his friend and a final characterization of the sort of love for the world he has been talking about:

A Regulated well orderd Lov Upon Clear Causes, and with a Rational Affection, guided to Divine and Celestial Ends. Which is to lov with a Divine and Holy Lov, Glorious and Blessed. We are all Prone to Love, but the Art lies in Managing our Love: to make it truly Amiable and Proportionable. To lov for GODS sake, and to this End, that we may be Wel Pleasing unto Him: to lov with a Design to imitate Him, and to satisfy the Principles of Intelligent Nature and to becom Honorable: is to lov in a Blessed and Holy maner. (69)

Traherne's design for this imitation is the path we have just followed, a reflection and communion in the human soul based on the nature of all things as they exist in terms of the progression of estates of being, a progression that can be known and loved because it is a successive line of development permanent in all its parts. Knowing the world in terms of these estates removes the first veil from the temple of Glory.

NOTES

1. Isabel G. MacCaffrey, "The Meditative Paradigm," *ELH*, XXXII (1965) , 395.

2. *The Eloquent "I"*, p. 267.

3. Martz says that this section "introduces the primary symbol of his *Centuries*: Adam in Paradise becomes the symbol of all the possibilities still resident within redeemed mankind" (p. 60) . This application is too broad. Adam in Paradise is primary only in the parts treating the estate of Innocence, and is superceded both in the work and in Traherne's thought by that for which it itself is a symbol or type, Christ.

VI

The Journey Inward

The *Centuries* are about the soul's journey to Glory, to a knowledge and love of all things in eternity and time. The *Centuries* themselves also are that journey, for form and content become one in this work. What we have followed so far has been the journey in terms of the outer world. Traherne now turns to deal with the same development in terms of the inner world, that world within the soul of each man. Though the directions of the journey outward and the journey inward are different, the means and ends are the same. These twin journeys are treated by Traherne in this particular order both because the inner world is the more important of the two (Traherne always develops his ideas climactically), and because this order reflects Traherne's theory of learning—that the soul can be filled with ideas only by internal assimilation of things first found outside itself. Because the two journeys are through parallel areas of being to the same end, we can expect Traherne's method of development in treating this second one to be similar to that used with the first. Many previously developed ideas and forms (i.e., the journey through the four estates) are repeated here but with variety in their presentation and in terms more suited to the treatment of the individual soul.

Brooding over this part, and over all the *Centuries*, is Traherne's concept of eternity-time as a successive development of which all parts are always in existence. It could be said that Traherne, in the *Centuries*, is always talking about everything. The journey outward and the journey inward are the same journey, one that covers all the ground there is. Nothing can be treated in isolation, because any one major part of being, the world for instance, includes both of the others, man and God.

97

Each of these three is by presence or reflection included in the others. However, the simultaneous aspect of all this does not lead to a confused presentation precisely because of the successive nature seen in the development of things in eternity-time. There exists a pattern, a pattern which, however, can be seen from different points of view and which is a growth that does not leave the old behind but expands to include more and more until it has all.

In Century II, 70, the point of view shifts from a contemplation of the outer world and its many souls to one of the inner world of one soul:

> In the Soul of Man there are innumerable Infinities. One Soul in the Immensity of its Intelligence, is Greater and more Excellent then the whole World The Ocean is but the Drop of a Bucket to it, the Heavens but a Centre, the Sun Obscurity, and all Ages but as one Day. It being by its Understanding a Temple of Eternity, and GODS Omnipresence. between which and the whole World there is no Proportion.   (70)

Traherne reaffirms his belief that we need others, but this is now presented as a need to see the reflection of ourselves in those others and thus "liv again in other Persons" (70). He goes on to speak of the power of the individual soul to be present not only with other people but with all the rest of the creation as well (71), an achievement impossible on this earth, "but in Heaven where the Soul is all Act it is necessary" (73).

Traherne quotes Revelation to demonstrate the multitude of things that will be available to the soul in Glory (74-75). He stresses the inward nature of this experience. What the soul will see in Glory could never be seen, as most things of this world could, "with your Bodily Eys" (76). Of the objects perceived in Glory,

> You shall be present with them in your Understanding. You shall be In them to the very centre and they in you. As Light is in a Piece of Chrystal, so shall you be with every Part and Excellency of them. An Act of the Understanding is the presence of the Soul, which being no Body but a Living Act, is a Pure Spirit, and Mysteriously fathomless in its true Dimensions.   (76)

Here on earth we work toward this by holding in our understanding all the created things among which we live. We must not be lazy in this but should actively seek out our "Riches" in all places in order that we may add them to our understanding.

Traherne shows that the inner world is like the outer one. He illustrates one aspect of this with the example of rays of light which, unless they strike an object, have no means of showing their existence; just so the soul, if it lacked the objects toward which its understanding is directed, would have no demonstrable being (78). Thus we can see how inimical any mystic "negative way," clearing the mind of its particular objects, would have been to this hoarder of knowledge.

Because of the nature of our souls, love can fill eternity and immensity by its presence with the objects there; yet each soul does this completely within itself (80). This inner infinity of the soul is the first thing a child knows; this feeling, at least, may be innate:

> That things are finit therfore we learn by our Sences. but Infinity we know and feel by our Souls: and feel it so Naturaly, as if it were the very Essence and Being of the Soul. The truth of it is, It is individualy in the Soul: for GOD is there, and more near to us then we are to our selvs. So that we cannot feel our Souls, but we must feel Him, in that first of Properties infinit Space.   (81)

The infinite space Traherne is talking about is, of course, "inner" space: "What shall we render unto God for this infinit Space in our Understandings!" (82).

Thus God's treasures are not only infinite in extent (the outer world),

> but in Depth also they are evry where infinit being infinit in Excellency. And the Soul is a Miraculous Abyss of infinit Abysses, an Undrainable Ocean, an inexhausted fountain of Endles Oceans.   (83)

Given this infinite capacity of the soul, we are to fill it with ideas until it becomes the image of the all-knowing God; "For then shall we be *Mentes* as He is *Mens*. We being of the same Mind, with him who is an infinit Eternal mind" (84). This growth in knowledge makes our love more acceptable to God because it makes us more worthy to be loved; and such love eventually enables us to "appear before GOD in Sion: and as GOD convers with GOD for evermore" (86). In our love as in our knowledge, we are to make our souls like God. By maintaining the presence of all the world in our understandings, we imitate Him in His constant care for the world (87). In Glory it will be impossible not to do this (89).

In dealing with the outer world, Traherne had stressed the idea that the services of things were of far greater importance than the things themselves. Traherne now shows "that the Idea of Heaven and Earth in the Soul of Man, is more Precious with GOD then the Things them selvs" (90), the primary reason for this being that ideas are

> Spiritual and Nearer unto GOD. The Material World is Dead and feeleth Nothing. But this Spiritual World tho it be Invisible hath all Dimensions, and is a Divine and Living Being, the Voluntary Act of an Obedient Soul.   (90)

Building the world in your mind and holding it there, this is what the *Centuries* are all about. This act is "to see Eternity, to fill His Omnipresence . . . and to live in His Image" (92). This is a vision which flowers, as noted before, in praises and thanksgivings, "For Praises are Transformed and returning Benefits" (94). The greatest benefit for which we return praise is "the Lov of Jesus Christ" in restoring man to this vision of the world (95).

The world, then, is not only the outer creation: "The World is a Pomgranat indeed, which GOD hath put into mans Heart, as Solomon observeth in the Ecclesiastes, becaus it containeth the Seeds of Grace and the Seeds of Glory" (96). All the things philosophers ever proposed as the source of happiness meet together here in this knowledge of all things in the inner and outer worlds. Only the negative way cannot be accommodated. Traherne is contemptuous to those who would teach others to find happiness through restraints. Felicity comes from the proper direction of activity, not from the hindering of it. The end vision, eternity, may be stable but its stability is that of the ocean, a body of constant form filled with motion.

Traherne sums up his method for achieving felicity:

So that whosoever will Profit in the Mystery of Felicity, must see the Objects of His Happiness; and the Maner how they are to be Enjoyed, and discern also the Powers of His Soul by which He is to enjoy them, and perhaps the Rules that shall Guid Him in the Way of Enjoyment.   (100)

Traherne has dealt with the object and the means, he is now dealing with the powers of the soul and will deal with some rules in the Fourth Century. He goes on in the Third Century to retrace the "Maner how they are to be Enjoyed" that he had sketched in the Second Century, 1-69, this time in terms of one individual soul in its development through the estates, seeing in inner history what the "you" of the Second Century had seen in outer history and the external world.

The Third Century is an exercise in holding the internal world in the understanding, as Traherne calls back to mind the history of his intellectual development. The concern here is not with the objects that filled Traherne's world or even their services to the world as a whole; what is important here is the effect objects had on a growing mind. The line of development in this Century is chronological, but seen from a fixed point of view; the past is viewed in terms of knowledge the adult Traherne has gained since the time of the events he describes.

Most of the vision of this Century is simultaneously personal and universal. Traherne begins with infancy and childhood, but the infancy he recounts is that of human history as well as his own. "Certainly Adam in Paradice had not more sweet and Curious Apprehensions of the World, then when I was a child" (1).

All appeared New, and Strange at the first, inexpressibly rare, and Delightfull, and Beautifull. I was a little Stranger which at my Entrance into the World was Saluted and Surrounded with innumerable Joys. My Knowledg was Divine. I knew by Intuition those things which since my Apostasie, I Collected again, by the Highest Reason. My very Ignorance was Advantageous. I seemed as one Brought into the Estate of Innocence.   (2)

He "knew by Intuition" infinity and eternity, not thoughts and ideas, which were to come from things.

References to Adam and Eden recur throughout this treat-
ment of the estate of Innocence, a period when "All Time was
Eternity" (2). As a child, Traherne lived "in the Peace of
Eden; Heaven and Earth did sing my Creators Praises and could
not make more Melody to Adam, then to me" (2). "The
Citie seemed to stand in Eden, or to be Built in Heaven" (3).
These descriptions he gives to the world the child saw are
among the most popular of Traherne's prose writings. Here
again he stresses the importance of meditation on the estate of
Innocence as a starting point, for "He must be Born again and
becom a little Child that will enter into the Kingdom of Heav-
en" (5). We do this by putting the corruptions of the world so
far out of mind that "only those Things appear, which did to
Adam in Paradice, in the same Light, and in the same Colors"
(5).

Man falls away from his childlike vision and must work to
return to it. Tracing that return is the purpose of this Century.
"And by what Steps and Degrees I proceeded to that Enjoyment
of all Eternity which now I possess I will likewise shew you"
(6). Sections 7-14 deal almost exclusively with what Traherne elsewhere calls the estate of Misery, the soul after the fall
from its childhood innocence. It is notable that these sections
are almost empty of references to the larger vision which sees
the past and future in and through the present. Traherne does
see the corruption he is dealing with as deriving from Adam's
fall (8), and what he says of himself does apply to every man;
but the Biblical-historical applications and point of view are
largely missing. Here again we see the form reflecting the content, for in the estate of Misery the vision of eternity-time is
lost. While it would have been possible for Traherne, writing
from the point of view of one who knows what is at the end of
the journey, to include historical parallels in his usual manner,
it is more effective and illustrative that he does not do so. He
speaks of what the soul in Misery is confined to, present things:
"Tinsild Ware upon a Hobby hors" (9), the "Barbarous Inven-
tions" of the modern world which "put Grubs and Worms in
Mens Heads" (13) and to which he contrasts the lack of posses-
sions among the innocent "Barbarous Indians" (12).

Because many of the specific ideas presented in this Century
have already been noted and discussed in connection with earlier Centuries (though now they are being applied to the indi-

vidual soul), the survey of this Century can deal in broader terms with its general movement and development. Two things are of especial note: (1) how the Bible gains in importance as the soul's vision expands, and (2) how the treatment of topics becomes less personal and more universal.

Traherne makes it clear that the fall into Misery is a forgetting and a failure of the understanding: "I had utterly forgotten all Goodness Bounty Comfort and Glory: for lack of which therfore He was unknown" (14). But into the dark existence of Misery came Grace. It came first through dreams (15) and intuitions (16), but his thoughts were still confined. "I knew not then my Soul, or Body: nor did I think of the Heavens and the Earth, the Rivers and the Stars, the Sun or the Seas: all those were lost, and Absent from me" (16). Questions started to form in his mind, questions about those things which he knew to be in the world but of which he had no immediate knowledge through his senses. As he learned to think about unseen things, his soul's vision began to grow:

> Som times I should Soar abov the Stars and Enquire how the Heavens Ended, and what was beyond them? concerning which by no means could I receiv satisfaction. som times my Thoughts would carry me to the Creation, for I had heard now, that the World which at first I thought was Eternal, had a Beginning: how therfore that Beginning was, and Why it was; Why it was no sooner, and what was before; I mightily desired to Know. By all which I easily perceiv that my Soul was made to live in Communion with GOD, in all Places of his Dominion, and to be satisfied with the Highest Reason in all Things.   (18)

As he learned of the extent of his soul, Traherne also discovered the necessity for limits in the material world, finally finding "That infinit Worth shut up in the Limits of a Material Being, is the only way to a Real Infinity" (20). But his vision of the soul only began to form now and was "not atchieved till a long time afterwards" (22).

In the meantime he had experiences which, though also not fully understood until much later, prepared his soul for the truth it was to receive. One such experience was of seeing a room prepared for a feast, a fascinating sight which very soon, however, ceased to interest the child. When, later, he saw the

room filled with men and women, the place that had become
dull was transformed and there was "nothing of Tediousness
but pleasure in it" (22). From thinking of this experience he
learned how other people were needed for true happiness. He
also learned the value of motion above static forms. Another of
his experiences was that of being overcome by loneliness in an
empty field. He felt this experience came about through his
forgetting his involvement in all the universe (23).

However, what opened the way for the growing Traherne
more than anything else was his curiosity to learn new things
and the ability he found to create things, though he had never
seen them, in his imagination.

When I heard of any New Kingdom beyond the seas, the
Light and Glory of it pleased me immediatly, entered into
me, it rose up within me and I was Enlarged Wonderfully.
I entered into it, I saw its Commodities, Rarities, Springs,
Meadows, Riches, Inhabitan [t] s, and became Possessor of
that New Room, as if it had been prepared for me, so much
was I Magnified and Delighted in it.   (24)

It was the love of news that led Traherne to the good news of
the Bible. "When the Bible was read my Spirit was present in
other Ages . . . This shewd me the Liveliness of interior
presence, and that all Ages were for most Glorious Ends, Accessible to my Understanding" (24). He wanted to learn of new
things so much that he developed a desire for a book from
heaven (perhaps as a result of reading Revelation). But the
book, he found (like other readers of Revelation) was already
before him; it was the Bible. Traherne discusses this gift of the
Bible as he did that of Christ and of creation in previous
Centuries, by showing that a book from heaven could not have
come to him in any better way. God's method of giving him this
gift made it as universal as was possible.

But the Bible was not the only book from which Traherne
learned. At the university he studied many subjects. His studies
showed him how much there was in the world but did not show
him how all this pertained to his happiness. "There was never a
Tutor that did professely Teach Felicity" (37) says Traherne.
We must seek to learn both how our studies can be applied to
ourselves and also what they have to do with the nature of God.

Eventually, according to Traherne, these two considerations become one, when we see that man's happiness and God's Glory
are the same.

Traherne treats those specific areas of learning which he has
found to be of most importance, defining them in terms of the
knowledge they led him to rather than according to their usual
limits. These include Humanity, the study of the nature of the
soul; Divinity, the study of the essence of God and of man "in
his fourfold Estate" (43); Natural Philosophy, the inquiry into
the nature of all things; and Ethics, the study "of Moralitie, and
the Nature of Affections Virtues and Maners" (45). All of
these fields of study in their final stages become the same field,
for all lead to the God-like soul's knowledge and love of all
things.

From the university, Traherne went to live in the country;

> and being seated among silent Trees, had all my Time in
> mine own Hands, I resolved to Spend it all, whatever it cost
> me, in Search of Happiness, and to Satiat that burning Thirst
> which Nature had Enkindled, in me from my Youth.   (46)

His search was successful, and, speaking from the present, Traherne says he now finds himself living "a free and a Kingly Life,
as if the World were turned again into Eden, or much more,
as it is at this day" (46).

After first making a strong rejection of sin, such a rejection
being the prerequisite for a holy life, Traherne sketches the
method of contemplation he employed while in the country.
With so many objects for thought possible, he determined he
must choose only the best. The best things, he found, were "the
most Obvious and Common Things" (53). These include "Air,
Light, Heaven and Earth, Water, the Sun, Trees, Men and
Women, Cities, Temples &c." (53) as well as invisible things
such as "The Laws of God, the Soul of Man, Jesus Christ and
His Passion on the Crosse, with the Ways of GOD in all Ages"
(54). But after he had begun studying these obvious things

> to my unspeakable Wonder, they brought me to all the
> Things in Heaven and in Earth, in Time and Eternity, Pos-
> sible and Impossible, Great and Little, Common and Scarce,
> and Discovered them all to be infinit Treasures.   (54)

His method was to find the relationship the object of his thought had to eternity:

> That any thing may be found to be an infinit Treasure, its Place must be found in Eternity, and in Gods Esteem. For as there is a Time, so there is a Place for all Things. Evry thing in its Place is Admirable Deep and Glorious: out of its Place like a Wandering Bird, is Desolat and Good for Nothing. How therfore it relateth to God and all Creatures must be seen before it can be Enjoyed.   (55)

He found the ability to come to such knowledge through remembering that he had been created in the image of God. Traherne thus comes back to the condition he experienced in infancy, infinity, a condition characteristic of all of God's creatures since they are *"Almighty Power wholy exerted"* (62), eternal act. Not only are all things infinite, they are eternal.

> All Things being now to be seen and Contemplated in His Bosom: and Advanced therfore into a Diviner Light, being infinitly Older and more Precious then we were aware. Time itself being in GOD Eternaly.   (65)

This vision of things under the aspect of eternity is a vision of Glory, a communion with God, though Traherne says he was not aware of this when he first began to see things in this manner (66). What led him to discover that this was "the Way of Communion with God in all Saints" was "the Person of David" (66) as evidenced in the Psalms. As he read them, Traherne says, a light emanated from the Psalms which eventually threw light upon the entire Bible. He learned to look on the objects of his contemplations with eyes like David's, seeing them all as benefits to be returned to God through praise and thanksgiving.

The remainder of the Third Century is largely filled with quotations from the Psalms, they being, we recall, a type of the music of the New Jerusalem; and praises, according to Traherne, "the very End for which the World was created" (82) and the activity of the soul in Glory. David was able to praise as he did, to commune with God, "in the Light of Prophesie, not of History. Much more therfore should we rejoyce, who see these Prophesies fulfilled" (96). Through the study of God's working in time, his history, we can come to the vision of Glory.

From personal loss of vision Traherne has advanced through this Century to a glimpse, by the light of the Bible, into eternity and Glory.

The purpose of the Fourth Century is stated clearly at its opening:

> Having spoken so much concerning his Entrance and Progress in Felicity, I will in this Centurie speak of the Principles with which your friend endued Himself to enjoy it! for besides Contemplativ, there is an Activ Happiness; which consisteth in Blessed Operations. And as som things fit a man for Contemplation, so there are others fitting him for Action: which as they are infinitly necessary to Practical Happiness, so are they likewise infinitely conduciv to Contemplativ it self.   (1)

From contemplation of the journey through the estates, Traherne is turning to those principles which, when followed actively, make life happier and the fruition of contemplation possible. In keeping with the nature of the general subject, the soul, these are principles which apply to the activities of the individual. The Fourth Century might be said to mirror in a very general way the First Century. Both Centuries are primarily concerned with principles and ideas related to the road to Glory but do not present a detailed tracing of that road. Both culminate in a discussion of love, the First Century ending with a discussion of love for others as typified by the love of Jesus Christ, and the concluding portions of the Fourth Century dealing largely with self-love and with God's love for the individual soul. Louis Martz, in *The Paradise Within,* on page 100 sees this Century concerned with "the third stage of Bonaventure's journey," that in which "the mind is able to seek God by inquiring into the 'essential attributes' of God and into the 'properties' of the Trinity." Martz bases his argument largely on the discussion of love at the end of the Fourth Century. But the principles Traherne discusses, and the points of view from which love is treated (self-love, love of others, the love of God for the soul) are concerned, as my discussion in this chapter should make clear, with the individual soul, not with God directly.

In this Century Traherne speaks of the author of the previous Centuries in the third person, saying that this person taught the present speaker the things he is relating. Traherne does use the pronoun "I" in this Century, but it is not a lapse in his established point of view. "I" is the present speaker, representative of man in general, learning and having learned these things. The reason for this shift in point of view is not modesty, for Traherne says specifically that there is no immodesty involved in declaring one's principles:

I speak not His Practices but His Principles. I should too much Prais your friend did I speak his Practices, but it is no shame for any man to declare his Principles, tho they are the most Glorious in the world.   (30)

Traherne adds, wittily, that his friend did, however, ask him, because of modesty, to say of his practices that they were never willingly in violation of these principles.

This shift in point of view does, however, have a marked effect on the style, an effect which contributes greatly to the maintenance of Traherne's direction, purpose and unity. This change allows him to present the "I" of the Third Century somewhat as an idealized human being who has been advanced into the vision of Glory and who can thus deal with these principles always in terms of his success. By speaking of "his" principles, Traherne keeps our vision fixed on the end of the journey we are to make and emphasizes that the "I" of the last Century was not just Traherne but every man. Though these principles are things to be learned during the course of the journey to Glory, Traherne's use of the third person sustains this Century at the level on which the Third Century concluded.

Joan Webber, on pages 231 and 232 of *The Eloquent "I"*, explains this shift in terms of a link to the figure of David in the Third Century:

"In the third century, Traherne's identification with David, whom he still continues to speak of as 'he,' eases the transition to a separation of himself into a 'he' and an 'I' who play the same roles that 'David' and 'Traherne' do. The 'he,' or 'your Friend' of the fourth century is a rarified being who has achieved felicity at least partly through the Psalms, and who now through the mediation of the 'I' sends down principles to the reader, somewhat as God did through Moses to the children of the Hebrews."

Yet "identification" with David in the Third Century seems to be no more than the same sympathetic identification and communion felt with Adam and with Christ in the estates to which they belong. The role the "he" plays is not just that of David, but of Adam, of Christ, and of every human soul advanced to the vision of Glory. The separation is not that of God and Moses, but of Christ and the human soul which imitates and contains him.

We have already considered, in other contexts, several of the principles with which Traherne deals. Treated at length here is the principle that "evry man ought to spend his time, in studying diligently Divine Philosophy" (3), the study of which involves the contemplation of happiness and of universal things in a life of practiced virtue. Traherne stresses that felicity is to be sought here, not hereafter. Some other principles are that "*It is a Good Thing to be Happy alone*" (14), that the inner value of an object is more important than its being, and that one should communicate with the wisest and best of men. The principles of charity and of free will receive significant consideration also.

Several principles important in terms of our present study of Traherne's vision of eternity-time are to be found in this Century. For instance, Traherne says that the principle of charity is developed in the soul through the contemplation of Paradise:

He generaly held, that Whosoever would enjoy the Happiness of Paradice must put on the Charity of Paradice. . . . He called his Hous the Hous of Paradice: not only because it was the Place wherin he enjoyed the whole World, but because it was evry ones hous in the whole world. for observing the Methods, and studying the Nature of Charity in Paradice, he found that all men would be Brothers and Sisters throughout the whole World. and evermore love one another as their own selvs, tho they had never seen each other before.   (22)

"He thought the Stars as fair now, as they were in Eden, the sun as Bright, the Sea as Pure" (24); only man has fallen, but he may return. The same timeless vision is to be found in the principle "that he was to treat evry man in the Person of Christ. That is both as if Himself were Christ in the Greatnes of his Lov, and also as if the Man were Christ" (28).

Traherne deals with the estates in this Century also, listing principles he associates with them. He speaks of the innate goodness of creation and the dominion given man, man's ability to "receiv all the Things in Heaven and Earth" (50).

> If you ask, what is becom of us since the Fall? becaus all these things now lately named seem to pertain to the Estate of Innocency; Truly Now we have superadded Treasures: Jesus Christ. And are restored to the Exercise of the same Principles, upon higher Obligations.   (53)

Life according to its original principles can be brought about through self-love; for when we see, know and love ourselves as we truly are, created in God's image, capable of infinity and eternity, and loved so much by God that He "made the World and gav his Son" (58), we cannot help but see how others are made in the same image and equally worthy of love. Traherne says he spent "ten yeers studying before he could satisfy his Self Lov. And now finds nothing more easy then to lov others better than oneself" (55). This love of others is characteristic of the estate of Grace. We are to love all men as Christ did. "Is it unnatural to do what Jesus Christ hath don?" (59).

Yet Traherne never allows us to forget the result of his methods and principles, Glory. We are reminded that the heaven we seek is internal: "Tis not Change of Place, but Glorious Principles well Practiced that establish Heaven in the Life and Soul" (37). He calls up the picture of the "I" of the last Century, for whom "Having these Principles nothing was more easy then to enjoy the world. which being enjoyed, he had nothing more to do, then to spend his Life in Praises and Thanksgiving" (41). The full realization of Glory occurs after death, but we dare not put off the journey. "And remember that this and the other life are made of a Piece: but this is the time of Trial, that of Rewards" (60).

In section 61 Traherne, though he has been treating love before this point, decides to speak of it in a more direct way. "Since Lov will thrust in it self as the Greatest of all Principles, let us at last willingly allow it Room" (61). Love is identified as itself filled with principles "that would make me fit for all Ages" (66). This can come about because of the nature of love:

> It is present with all Objects, and Tasts all Excellencies, and meeteth the Infinitness of GOD in evry Thing. So that in Length it is infinit as well as in Bredth. . . . Thence also it can see into further Spaces, Things present and Things to come Hight and Depth being open before it, and all things in Heaven Eternity and Time equaly near.   (66)

This is, of course, the same thing Traherne has been saying about the natures of man and God; and Traherne explains that love, too, is "His Image" (67) and indeed "this Lov is your tru Self when you are in Act what you are in Power" (67). The soul in Glory is an act of love expressed in praise and thanksgiving for all things. The soul thus

> can Lov Adam in Eden, Moses in the Wilderness, Aaron in the Tabernacle, David before the Ark, S. Paul among the Nations, and Jesus either in the Manger or on the crosse All these it can love with violence. And when it is restored from all that is Terrene and Sensual, to its tru Spiritual Being, it can lov these and any of these as violently as any Person in the Living Age.   (67)

> To lov all Persons in all Ages, All Angels, all Worlds is Divine and Heavenly. To lov all Cities and all Kingdoms, all Kings and all Peasants, and evry Person in all Worlds with a natural intimat familiar Lov, as if Him alone, is Blessed. This makes a Man Effectualy Blessed in all Worlds, a Delightfull Lord of all Things, a Glorious friend to all Persons, a concerned Person in all Transactions, and ever present with all Affairs.   (69)
> The Omnipresence therfore and the Eternity of GOD are our Throne, wherin we are to reign for evermore.   (72)

Many similar quotations could be drawn out of the remainder of this Century. Traherne develops the idea of the soul's power to love infinity and eternity by means of a discussion of the mind's ability to accommodate itself to the size of any object it chooses to contemplate, by quotations from Pico and others, and by analogy to the powers of things in the physical universe such as the sun or a mirror. He stresses the necessity for the constant exercise of this power in order to develop it to its fullest capacity.

In the last section of this Century, Traherne lists the benefits which will derive from this expansion of the soul to its infinite capacity. As the last and most important one Traherne gives: "A Perfect Indwelling of the Soul in GOD, and GOD in the Soul" (100). It is now time to treat the end as it is in itself; it is time to consider directly the nature of God.

VII

The One

The Fifth Century consists of ten sections followed in the manuscript by the numeral "11" and forty-eight blank leaves. Though several of Traherne's recent critics maintain that the *Centuries* are complete, all of the nonemotional evidence seems to indicate otherwise. In his edition of Traherne's *Centuries*, H. M. Margoliouth says of the last section of this Century: "I cannot but look on V. 10 as a triumphant and perfect conclusion. How could Traherne have gone beyond it? The *Centuries* are not unfinished;" But he himself admits that the "11" following this section indicates "that Traherne, at one time at any rate, thought of going on" (I, xi). Traherne's decision never to continue could not have been made until after *C*, V, 10 was finished. Lacking external evidence, there is no sure proof that Traherne ever determined that he had finished the Fifth Century.

There is, of course, the presentation quatrain:

This book unto the friend of my best friend
As of the Wisest Love a Mark I send
That she may write my Makers prais therin
And make her self therby a Cherubin.

This has problems of its own. It is the sort of inscription one expects to find in a blank gift book, not in a book already nearly two-thirds full. This quatrain is not followed immediately by the *Centuries* in the manuscript but by what Margoliouth describes as "Notes by Traherne on Blessedness, a series of headings with no special connexion with the Centuries" (I, x). After this is a page on which is written, not in Traherne's hand,

113

the title, "Centuries of Meditations," followed by three blank pages. Then Traherne's *Centuries* begin. Thus the quatrain may have had nothing to do with the *Centuries*.

The strongest evidence that Traherne's intentions for the Fifth Century were never completed is the opening of that Century itself, where Traherne clearly states his purpose:

> The objects of Felicitie, and the Way of enjoying them, are two Material Themes; wherin to be instructed is infinitly desirable, becaus as Necessary, as Profitable. Whether of the Two, the Object, or the Way be more Glorious; it is difficult to determine. God it the Object, and God is the Way of Enjoying. God in all his Excellencies, Laws and Works, in all his Ways and Councels is the Soveraign Object of all Felicitie. Eternity and Time, Heaven and Earth, Kingdoms and Ages, Angels and Men, are in him to be enjoyed. In him, the fountain, in him the End; in him the Light, the Life, the Way, in him the Glory and Crown of all. Yet for Distinction sake, we will speak of several eminent Particulars. Beginning with the Attributes.   (1)

All things come together in God. Things do not lose their identity, they keep their "place", but the end of the journey we have been tracing is the soul's vision of all things included in God, who is still greater than all things. Traherne seems about to speak of many of the subjects he has touched on before; but here, once again, his direction of approach to these subjects will be different. He will speak of these things not so much in terms of the world or of the human soul, but as they exist in and from God.

Traherne wrote the *Centuries* not haphazardly but with certain organizational principles in mind. From what we have seen before, we can take him at his word that he intends this Century to be a discussion of the several things included under the concept of God, "Beginning with his Attributes." The nine sections remaining treat only three attributes: infinity, eternity and omnipresence. It is safe to assume that Traherne could not have intentionally finished a treatment of God's attributes without a discussion of love. Love of others had a crowning place in his meditation on the external world; self-love played a major role in his meditation on the soul. The Fifth Century is missing a consideration of love as an attribute of God as well as consid-

erations of whatever other "eminent Particulars" Traherne had
in mind.

Of the attributes he does consider, Traherne says that God's
infinity is to be enjoyed because it "comprehends infinit Space"
(2) where all treasures are to be found, because by means of it
we are capable of enlarging our thoughts without bounds, and
because it not only surrounds us but fills us as well and is thus
more easily known than anything physical. Because of God's
infinity, His goodness and all of His other characteristics are
infinite. Infinite space "is like a Painters Table" (5) filled with
everything that could possibly be painted on it. But there is an
infinity which surrounds this picture, one present to the inner
"Ey" which sees infinity in its eternal aspect.

And thus we are brought to the attribute of eternity.

> Eternity is a Mysterious Absence of Times and Ages: an
> Endless Length of Ages always present, and for ever Perfect.
> For as there is an immovable Space wherin all finit Spaces are
> enclosed, and all Motions carried on, and performed: so is
> there an Immovable Duration, that contains and mea-
> sures all moving Durations. Without which first the last
> could not be.   (7)

All beginnings and endings, all thoughts and acts, all souls are
before God and in His eternity.

Finally, God's omnipresence makes Him present with us everywhere and we with Him. Being present with the omnipresent God places us in the company of everything that is.
God's presence and consequently our participation in it has
nothing of a static nature. We have seen the importance of
movement in Traherne before, and this importance arises because God is "a Pure and simple Act" and thus His being

> is present in its Operations, and by those Acts which it eter-
> naly exerteth, is wholly Busied in all Parts and places of his
> Dominion, perfecting and compleating our Bliss and Hap-
> piness.   (10)

After this comes the numeral "11" and those blank pages that
one reader, at least, has taken to symbolize the height of a
mystic state of repose. Some of Traherne's "Thanksgivings" may
indicate where the Fifth Century would have gone. Certain-

ly the "Thanksgivings for God's Attributes" must, at any rate,
be taken into account. These "Thanksgivings" of Traherne's are
prayers of petition and, mainly, of praise. They are in form
similar to contemporary Psalm translations and are especially
like the *Private Devotions* of Lancelot Andrewes, a parallel
noted by Carol Marks. They deal with many of the subjects
mentioned in *C*, V, 1 as well as with the body and the soul;
there is also "A Thanksgiving and Prayer for the NATION."

In the "Thanksgivings for God's Attributes," Traherne, after
praises of the God who

> . . . hath made my Soul
> In the Image of himself,
> An understanding eye,
> That like an open day,
> Shall at once be present in all places,
> (9-13)

speaks of the many attributes of God now visible to him. He
deals especially with wisdom, goodness and power, and then
goes on to treat the three we saw discussed in the Fifth Century,
"Thine infinity, thine eternity, the exquisite perfection of
thine Omnipresence" (86-87). Eternity plays the greatest part
of the three, for it opens to vision the presence of God's love to
all possible things in all ages. Traherne desires while here on
earth to return in some measure the love that has been given
him.

The "Thanksgivings for the Wisdom of his WORD" are also of
especial interest to us. It is God's word that both shows us the
right way back to our true nature and provides us with proof
that we have reached our goal. God's word is

> A Book which thou hast sent
> To me from Heaven,
> (Detect the vanities of this wicked World,
> To ⟨ Guide my feet into the way of peace,
> (Shew me the Treasures of eternal Happiness.
> To Elevate my thoughts,   Purifie my heart,
> Enlighten my eyes,   Refine my Soul,
> Direct my Desires,   Quicken my Affections,
> Set my Mind in frame,   Restore me to thine Image,

Call me again to Communion with Thee,
In all thy Goods and Treasures.

(135-145)

The "word" is specifically the Bible, of course; the meaning
goes beyond application to that book.

Other of the "Thanksgivings" deal with God's providence, his
laws, and his works and ways. All are like the Fifth Century
in dealing with their subject in terms of God although, as
always, applications to man and the world are also present. The
progress Traherne has been treating is a cumulative one and its
end is clear; as he says in the *Meditations on the Six Days of the
Creation*, "We can never rest till we see all things from God
to God, proceeding from him, and ending in him" (p. 82).

In spite of variety in methods of presentation, Traherne's
message is usually the same. We have been dealing primarily
with *Christian Ethicks* and the *Centuries* in this study. The
concepts and methods of these works and even many of their
images occur also in Traherne's poetry, in the "Select Meditations" and in the *Meditations on the Six Days of the Creation*.

Louis Martz, in *The Paradise Within*, has commented on
repetition in the *Centuries*, showing its function in establishing
the contents of a meditation in the mind of the meditator. But
repetition in Traherne is as much related to his philosophy as it
is to his method of meditation. Traherne was striving for a
vision of the One; but the One, for Traherne, included the
many. The One is a statue of flawless marble, around which
Traherne leads his reader, pointing out its details and beauties
from one aspect, then another. At last he asks that we stand back
and see the work as a whole. The parts are of the same
material as the whole, though they differ in form. Every part
reflects the qualities characteristic of the whole in a relationship
that is mutual, for the qualities of the whole exist because of
their presence in the parts. The One, however, is not completely
like this statue, for the One is infinite and eternal, and thus all
its attributes are infinite and eternal. Form for it is not a physical property but a spiritual state of being.

Traherne chose to present his message in the variety of ways
he did in order to make it as clear as possible. The purpose of
his art was to teach. It also served as a matter of record; for, as
Martz notes, by recording those thoughts he felt to be essential

to the understanding of the One, he was helping to engrave them in his mind. The One must be seen from all possible points of view. That statement is as true of his art as it is of his philosophy. Traherne's life-problem was to find the possible ways of approaching truth.

Bibliography

I. Traherne Criticism (excluding brief mentions, editions of Traherne's works, literary histories and most reviews)

Ames, Kenneth J. "The Religious Language of Thomas Traherne's Centuries" (dissertation, University of Southern California, 1967). Abstracted in *Dissertation Abstracts*, XXVIII (1967), 3173A.

Barnstone, W. "Two Poets of Felicity: Thomas Traherne and Gorge Guillén," *Books Abroad*, XLII (1968), 14-19.

Beachcroft, T. O. "Traherne and the Cambridge Platonists," *Dublin Review*, CLXXXVI (1930), 278-290.

————. "Traherne and the Doctrine of Felicity," *The Criterion*, IX (1930), 291-307.

Bennett, J. A. W. "Traherne and Brasenose," *Notes and Queries*, CLXXXIX (1945), 84.

Bethell, S. L. *The Cultural Revolution of the Seventeenth Century*. New York, 1951.

Bicket, Zenos Johan. "An Imagery Study in Thomas Traherne's Centuries of Meditations" (dissertation, University of Arkansas, 1966). Abstracted in *Dissertation Abstracts*, XXVI (1966), 4624.

Bodleian Library. "The Manuscripts of Thomas Traherne," *Bodleian Library Record*, III (1951), 179-180.

Bottrall, Margaret. "Traherne's Praise of the Creation," *Critical Quarterly*, I (1959), 126-133.

Bury, R. G. "A Passage in Traherne," letter to *London Times Literary Supplement*, June 8, 1940, p. 279.

Cappuzzo, Marcello. "Thomas Traherne ('Poems' e 'Centuries of Meditation')," *Rendiconti*, XCVIII (1964), 69-88.

Christ, Ernst. *Studien zu Thomas Traherne*. Tübingen, 1932.

Clements, Arthur Leo. *The Mystical Poetry of Thomas Traherne*. Cambridge, Mass., 1969.

————. [Same Title], (dissertation, Syracuse, 1964). Abstracted in *Dissertation Abstracts*, XXV (1964), 1189.

————. "On the Mode and Meaning of Traherne's Mystical Poetry: 'The Preparative'," *Studies in Philology*, LXI (1964), 500-521.

Colby, Frances L. "Thomas Traherne and Henry More," *Modern Language Notes*, LXII (1947), 490-492.

————. "Traherne and the Cambridge Platonists: An Analytical Comparison," (dissertation, Johns Hopkins, 1948).

Colie, Rosalie L. *Paradoxia Epidemica*. Princeton, 1966.

————. "Thomas Traherne and the Infinite: The Ethical Compromise," *Huntington Library Quarterly*, XXI (1957), 69-82.

Connoly, Brian W. "Knowledge and Love: Steps Toward Felicity in Thomas Traherne," (dissertation, Pittsburg, 1966). Abstracted in *Dissertation*

119

Abstracts, XXVIII (1967) , 1047.

Daniells, Roy. "The Mannerist Element in English Literature," *University of Toronto Quarterly*, XXXVI (1966) , 1-11.

Dawson, M. L. "Thomas Treherne" [*sic*], letter to *London Times Literary Supplement*, September 29, 1927, p. 667.

Day, Malcom M. "Thomas Traherne and the Perennial Philosophy," (dissertation, Western Reserve, 1964) .

————. "Traherne and the Doctrine of Pre-existence," *Studies in Philology*, LXV (1968) , 81-98.

Denonian, Jean-Jaques. *Thèmes et Formes de la Poésie "Metaphysique."* Paris, 1956.

Diehm, Arnold. "Studien zu Mystik und Weltwirklich Keit in der Dichtung Andrew Marvells, Henry Vaughans, und Thomas Trahernes," (dissertation, Tübingen, 1957) .

Dobell, Bertram. "An Unknown Seventeenth Century Poet," *The Athenaeum* (April 7, 1900) , pp. 433-435.

Dobell, P. J. "A Passage in Traherne," letter to *London Times Literary Supplement*, June 15, 1940, p. 291.

Doughty, W. L. *Studies in Religious Poetry of the Seventeenth Century*. London, 1946.

Ellrodt, Robert. *L'Inspiration Personnelle et L'Esprit du Temps chez Les Poètes Métaphysiques Anglais*. Part I, vol. II. Paris, 1960.

————. "Le Message de Thomas Traherne," *Cahiers du Sud*, no. 31 (1950) , 434-456.

Fleming, William Kaye. *Mysticism in Christianity*. London, 1913.

Gilbert, Allan H. "Thomas Traherne as Artist," *Modern Language Quarterly*, VIII (1947) , 319-341, 435-447.

Goldknopf, David. "The Disintegration of Symbol in a Meditative Poet," *College English*, XXX (1968) , 48-59.

Grandvoinet, Renée. "Thomas Traherne and the Doctrine of Felicity," *Études de Lettres*, XIII (1939) , 164-177.

Grigson, Geoffrey. "The Transports of Thomas Traherne," *Bookman*, LXXXII (1932) , 250.

Guffey, George R. "Thomas Traherne on Original Sin," *Notes and Queries*, XIV (1967) , 98-100.

————. "Margoliouth's Emendation of a Line in Traherne's 'For Man to Act'," *American Notes and Queries*, V (1967) , 162-163.

Hall, Rev. William C. "Poetical Works of Thomas Traherne," *The Manchester Quarterly*, XXIII (1904) , 376-382.

Harrison, Thomas P. "Seneca and Traherne," *Arion*, VI (1967) , 403-405.

Hepburn, Ronald W. "Thomas Traherne: The Nature and Dignity of Imagination," *The Cambridge Journal*, VI (1953) , 725-734.

Herman, E. *The Meaning and Value of Mysticism*. London, 1916.

Hobhouse, S. "A Poet's Resurrection," *Spectator*, CLVII (1936) , 804.

Hodgson, Geraldine E. *English Mystics*. London, 1922.

Hopkinson, Arthur W. "Thomas Traherne," letter to *London Times Literary Supplement*, October 6, 1927, p. 694.

Howarth, R. G. " 'Felicity' in Traherne," *Notes and Queries*, CXCIII (1948) , 249-250.

Huntington, Virginia E. "Thomas Traherne, Priest, Mystic, Poet," *Living Church*, no. 109 (1944) , 13-14.

Iredale, Queenie. *Thomas Traherne*. Oxford, 1935.

Itrat-Husain. *The Mystical Element in the Metaphysical Poets of the Seventeenth Century*. Edinburgh, 1948.

Jennings, Elizabeth. "The Accessible Art. A Study of Thomas Traherne's Centuries of Meditations," *Twentieth Century*, CLXVII (1960), 140-151.
Jones, Rufus M. *Spiritual Reformers in the 16th & 17th Centuries*. London, 1914.
Jones, W. Lewis. "Thomas Traherne and the Religious Poetry of the Seventeenth Century," *The Quarterly Review*, CC (1904), 437-464.
Korte, Donald M. "Thomas Traherne's 'The Estate,'" *Thoth*, VI (1965), 13-19.
Leishman, James Blair. *The Metaphysical Poets: Donne, Herbert, Vaughan, Traherne*. Oxford, 1934.
Lock, Walter. "An English Mystic," *The Constructive Quarterly*, I (1913), 826-836.
Löhrer, Frieda. *Die Mystic und ihre Quellen in Thomas Traherne*. Zürich, 1930.
McAdoo, Henry Robert. *The Spirit of Anglicanism*. London, 1965.
MacCaffrey, Isabel G. "The Meditative Paradigm," *ELH*, XXXII (1965), 388-407.
Macaulay, Rose. *Some Religious Elements in English Literature*. London, 1931.
Mahood, M. M. *Poetry and Humanism*. London, 1950.
Margoliouth, H. M. "Traherne's Ordination and Birth-Date," *Notes and Queries*, CXCIX (1954), 408.
Marks, Carol Louise. "Thomas Traherne and Hermes Trismegistus," *Renaissance News*, XIX (1966), 118-131.
_____. "Thomas Traherne's Commonplace Book," *Papers of the Bibliographical Society of America*, LVIII (1964), 458-465.
_____. "Thomas Traherne's Early Studies," *Papers of the Bibliographical Society of America*, LXII (1968), 511-536.
_____. "Traherne's Church's Year-Book," *Papers of the Bibliographical Society of America*, LX (1966), 31-72.
_____. "Thomas Traherne and Cambridge Platonism," *PMLA*, LXXXI (1966), 521-534.
_____. See also Sicherman, Carol Marks.
Marshall, William H. "Thomas Traherne and the Doctrine of Original Sin," *Modern Language Notes*, LXXIII (1958), 161-165.
Martz, Louis, L. *The Paradise Within: Studies in Vaughan, Traherne and Milton*. New Haven, 1964.
Massingham, Harold. "A Note on Thomas Traherne," *New Statesman*, IV (1914), 271-272.
More, Paul Elmer. "Thomas Traherne," *The Nation*, LXXXVIII (1909), 160-162.
Naylor, E. W. "Three Seventeenth Century Poet-Parsons and Music," *Proceedings of the Musical Association*, 55th session (1927-1928), 93-113.
Nicolson, Marjorie Hope. *The Breaking of the Circle*. New York, 1960.
Nomachi, Susumu. "Thomas Traherne," *Studies in English Literature* (Tokyo), XXIV (1945), 154-168.
Osborn, James M. "A New Traherne Manuscript," *London Times Literary Supplement*, October 8, 1964, p. 928.
Owen, Catherine A. "The Authorship of 'Meditations on the Six Days of Creation' and the 'Meditations and Devotions on the Life of Christ'," *Modern Language Review*, LVI (1961), 1-12.
Parker, S. T. H. "The Riches of Thomas Traherne," *Living Age*, CCCXIV (1922), 223-225.
Payne, Arthur. "A Prose Poet: Thomas Traherne," *Educational Times*,

122 THE TEMPLE OF ETERNITY

LXXIV (1922), 223-225.
Price, C. "Thomas Traherne," a letter to the *London Times Literary Supplement,* October 27, 1927, p. 767.
Proud, J. W. "Thomas Traherne: A Divine Philosopher," *Friends' Quarterly Examiner,* no. 201 (1917), 65-82.
Quiller-Couch, Sr. A. T. *From a Cornish Window.* Cambridge, 1906.
————. *Studies in Literature,* I. Cambridge, 1918.
Ridler, A. "Traherne: Some Wrong Attributions," *Review of English Studies,* XVIII (1967), 48-49.
Ridlon, Harold G. "The Function of the 'Infant-ey' in Traherne's Poetry," *Studies in Philology,* LXI (1964), 627-639.
Rostvig, Maren-Sofie. *The Happy Man,* vol. I. Oslo, 1954.
Rowley, Victor. "Thomas Traherne's *Centuries* and Aristotle's Theory of Change," (M. A. thesis, Ohio State University, 1967).
Russell, Angela. "The Life of Thomas Traherne," *Review of English Studies,* VI (1955), 34-43.
————. "A Study of Thomas Traherne's Christian Ethicks," (B. Litt. thesis, Oxford, 1952).
Salter, K. W. "The Date of Traherne's Ordination," *Notes and Queries,* CXCIX (1954), 282.
————. "The Nature of Traherne's Mysticism," (Master's thesis, Bristol, 1954).
————. *Thomas Traherne: Mystic and Poet.* New York, 1964.
————. "Traherne and a Romantic Heresy," *Notes and Queries,* CC (1955), 153-156.
Sandbank, S. "Thomas Traherne on the Place of Man in the Universe," *Studies in English Language and Literature,* ed. Alice Shalvi and A. A. Mendilow. Jerusalem, 1966.
Sauls, Lynn. "The Careless Compositor for *Christian Ethicks.*" *Papers of the Bibliographical Society of America,* LXIII (1969), 123-126.
Sayers, Dorothy L. "The Beatrician Vision in Dante and Other Poets," *Nottingham Mediaeval Studies,* II (1958), 3-23.
Seetaraman, M. W. "The Way of Felicity in Thomas Traherne's 'Centuries' and 'The Poems' " in *Critical Essays on English Literature,* ed. V. S. Seturaman. Madras, 1965.
Sherer, Gertrude R. "More and Traherne," *Modern Language Notes,* XXXIV (1919), 49-50.
Sicherman, Carol Marks. "Traherne's Ficino Notebook," *Papers of the Bibliographic Society of America,* LXIII (1969), 73-81.
————. See also Marks, Carol Louise.
Spurgeon, C. F. E. *Mysticism in English Literature.* Cambridge, 1913.
Staley, Thomas F. "The Theocentric Vision of Thomas Traherne," *Cithara,* IV (1964), 43-47.
Stranks, Charles James. *Anglican Devotion.* London, 1961.
Tanner, Lawrence Melvin. "Thomas Traherne's *Centuries of Meditations*: A Critical Introduction with Annotations for the *First* and *Second Centuries*" (dissertation, New York University, 1959). Abstracted in *Dissertation Abstracts,* XX (1960), 3310-3311.
Thompson, Elbert N. S. "The Philosophy of Thomas Traherne," *Philological Quarterly,* VIII (1929), 97-112.
Towers, Frances. "Thomas Traherne: His Outlook on Life," *The Nineteenth Century and After,* LXXXVII (1920), 1024-1030.
Uphaus, Robert. "Thomas Traherne: Perception as Process," *University of Windsor Review,* II (1968), 19-21.

Wade, Gladys I. "The Manuscripts of the Poems of Thomas Traherne,"
    Modern Language Review, XXVI (1931) , 401-407.
————. "Mrs. Susanna Hopton," *The English Review,* LXII (1936) , 41-
    47.
————. "St. Thomas Aquinas and Thomas Traherne," *Blackfriars,* XII
    (1931) , 666-673.
————. *Thomas Traherne: A Critical Biography.* Princeton, 1944.
————. "Thomas Traherne as 'Divine Philosopher'," *The Hibbert Journal,*
    XXXII (1934) , 400-408.
————. "Traherne and the Spiritual Value of Nature Study," *The London
    Quarterly and Holborn Review,* CLIX (1934) , 243-245.
Wahl, Jean. "Thomas Traherne: Poémes," *Mesures,* April 15, 1936, pp.
    59-82.
————. "Thomas Traherne," *Études Anglaises,* XIV (1961) , 116-126.
Wallace, John Malcolm. "Thomas Traherne and the Structure of Medita-
    tion," *ELH,* XXV (1958) , 79-89.
Watkins, Alfred. "Thomas Traherne," letter to *London Times Literary
    Supplement,* October 20, 1927, p. 742.
Webb, William. "Thomas Traherne's Poem 'Silence'," *Notes and Queries,* X
    (1964) , 96.
Webber, Joan. *The Eloquent "I": Style and Self in Seventeenth-Century
    Prose.* Madison, 1968.
————. " 'I' and 'Thou' in the Prose of Thomas Traherne," *Papers in
    Language and Literature,* II (1966) , 258-264.
White, Helen C. *The Metaphysical Poets: A Study in Religious Experience.*
    New York, 1936.
Wilde, Hans O. *Beiträge zur Englischen Literaturgeschichte des 17 Jahrhun-
    derts.* Breslau, 1932.
Willcox, Louise Collier. "A Joyous Mystic," *North American Review,*
    CXCIII (1911) , 893-904.
Willett, Gladys E. "Traherne," *Spectator,* CXXIV (1920) , 84-85.
————. *Traherne (An Essay)* . Cambridge, 1919.
Williams, Melvin G. "Thomas Traherne: Center of God's Wealth," *Cithara,*
    III (1963) , 32-40.
Willson, Cecil H. S. "Traherne and Wordsworth," *London Quarterly and
    Holborn Review,* July, 1939, pp. 355-358.
Willy, Margaret. *Life Was Their Cry.* London, 1950.
————. "Thomas Traherne: 'Felicity's Perfect Lover'," *English,* XII
    (1959) 210-215.
————. *Three Metaphysical Poets.* London, 1961.
Wilson, A. Doris L. "A Neglected Mystic: Thomas Traherne," *Poetry
    Review,* XVI (1925) , 11-22, 97-104, 178-182.
Winterbottom, K. M. "Certain Affinities to Wordsworth in the Poetry of
    Vaughan and Traherne," (dissertation, Pittsburg, 1933) .

II. Works Cited (other than those included above)

Traherne's Works

Centuries of Meditation, ed. Bertram Dobell. London, 1927.
Centuries, Poems, and Thanksgivings, ed. H. M. Margoliouth. 2 Vol.
    Oxford, 1958 [1965 reprint].
Christian Ethics, ed. Carol L. Marks and George Robert Guffey. Ithaca,
    New York, 1968.

"Ficino Notebook." British Museum MS. Burney 126.
Meditations on the Six Days of the Creation, ed. George Robert Guffey. Los Angeles, 1966.
Roman Forgeries. London, 1673.
"Select Meditations." MS. in the Osborn Collection, Yale University Library.

Other

Anselm. Saint Anselm: Basic Writings, trans. S. N. Deane. La Salle, Illinois, 1962 [orig. 1903].
————. "Proslogion" in A Scholastic Miscellany: Anselm to Ockham, ed. and trans. Eugene R. Fairweather in The Library of Christian Classics, ed. John Baille et al., X. London, 1956.
Aquinas, Thomas. St. Thomas Aquinas: Philosophical Texts, ed and trans. Thomas Gilby. London, 1951.
Augustine. The City of God, trans. Marcus Dods, II. New York, 1948.
————. The Confessions of Saint Augustine, [Modern Library ed.] trans. E. B. Pusey. New York, 1949.
————. "The Eight Questions of Dulcitus," in Saint Augustine: Treatises on Various Subjects, trans. Sister Mary Sarah Muldowney et al., in The Fathers of the Church, ed. Roy Joseph Deferrari, XIV. New York, 1952.
The Authorised Version of the English Bible 1611, ed. William Aldis Wright, V. Cambridge, 1909.
Barrow, Isaac. The Works of the Learned Isaac Barrow, D. D. London, 1683.
Bartlet, John. The Practical Christian. London, [1670].
Boethius. Boethius, The Theological Tractates, [Loeb ed.], trans. H. F. Stewart and E. K. Rand. Cambridge, Mass., 1962.
————. Consolation of Philosophy, trans. "I. T.," ed. William Anderson. Carbondale, Illinois, 1963.
Bramhall, John. The Catching of Leviathan in The Works of . . . John Bramhall. Dublin, 1676.
Bréhier, Émile. The History of Philosophy: The Seventeenth Century, trans. Wade Baskin. Chicago, 1966.
Callahan, John J. Four Views of Time in Ancient Philosopy. Cambridge, Mass., 1948.
Charron, Pierre. Of Wisdome Three Bookes, trans. Samson Lennard. London, 1640.
Crane, Ronald. "Anglican Apologetics and The Idea of Progress, 1699-1745," Modern Philology, XXXI (1934), 273-306, 349-382.
Crollius, Oswald. A Treatise of Oswaldus Crollius of Signatures of Internal Things. London, 1669.
Cudworth, Ralph. True Intellectual System of the Universe, II. London, 1845.
Daniélou, Jean. From Shadows to Reality, trans. Dom Wulstan Hibberd. Westminster, Maryland, 1960.
————. The Lord of History: Reflections on the Inner Meaning of History, trans. Nigel Abercrombie. London, 1958.
Davies, W. D. Paul and Rabbinic Judaism. London, 1965.
Dowden, Edward. "Elizabethan Psychology," Atlantic Monthly, C (1907), 388-399.
Fairburn, Patrick. The Typology of Scripture. Edinburgh, 1854.
Gale, Theophilus. Court of the Gentiles. Four Parts. London, 1669-1678.

Grant, R. M. *The Letter and The Spirit*. London, 1957.
Gregory of Nyssa. *Against Eunomius*, in *Nicene and Post-Nicene Fathers*, ed. Philip Schall and Henry Wace, V. Grand Rapids, Michigan, 1954 [American Reprint].
Guild, William, *Moses Unvailed*. London, 1620.
Hallet, H. F. *Benedict de Spinoza: The Elements of His Philosophy*. London, 1957.
Hobbes. *Leviathan*, [Everyman ed.], intro. A. D. Lindsay. New York, 1950.
Irenaeus. *The Ante-Nicene Fathers*, trans. Alexander Roberts and James Donaldson, I. Grand Rapids, Michigan, 1950. [American Reprint].
Jayne, Sears R. *John Colet and Marsilio Ficino*. Oxford, 1963.
_____. *Marsilio Ficino's Commentary on Plato's Symposium*. Columbia, Missouri, 1944.
Jackson, Thomas. *Treatise of the Divine Essence and Attributes*. London, 1628.
Keach, Benjamin. *Tropes and Figures*. London, 1682.
Kristeller, Paul Oskar. *The Philosophy of Marsilio Ficino*, trans. Virginia Conant. Gloucester, Mass., 1964.
Lampe, G. W. H. and K. J. Woolcombe. *Essays on Typology* [Studies in Biblical Theology, No. 22] 3. Naperville, Illinois, 1957.
[Mackenzie, George]. *Religio Stoici*. Edinburgh, 1665.
Madsen, William G. *From Shadowy Types to Truth*. New Haven, 1968.
Meyerhoff, Hans. *Time in Literature*. Berkeley, 1955.
More, Henry. *An Explanation of the Grand Mystery of Godliness*. London, 1660.
_____. *Antimonopsychia, or That all Souls are not one*, in *Psychodia Platonica*. Cambridge, 1642.
_____. *Divine Dialogues*, I. London, 1668.
_____. *Psychozoia*. Cambridge, 1642.
Parmenides. *Parmenides*, trans. and ed. Leonardo Taran. Princeton, 1965.
Plato. *The Dialogues of Plato*, trans. B. Jowett. New York, 1937.
Plotinus. *Enneads*, trans. Stephen MacKenna. New York, [1956].
Reynolds, Edward. *Treatise of the Passions and Faculties of the Soule of Man*. London, 1640.
Seneca. *Seneca's Letters to Lucilius*, trans. E. Phillips Barker. Oxford, 1932.
South, Robert. *Sermons Preached Upon Several Occasions*, I. Philadelphia, 1850.
Spinoza. *Spinoza's Ethics*, [Everyman ed.], trans. Andrew Boyle. London, 1910.
Staudenbaur, C. A. "Galileo, Ficino and Henry More's Psychathanasia," *Journal of the History of Ideas*, XXIX (1968), 565-578.
Stern, Madeline B. "Counter-clockwise: Flux of Time in Literature," *Sewanee Review*, XLIV (1936), 338-365.
Suter, Ronald. "Augustine on Time, With Some Criticisms from Wittgenstein," *Revue Internationale de Philosophie*, XVI (1962), 378-394.
Theologia Germanica, trans. Susanne Winkworth. New York, 1949.
Vaughan, Henry. *The Works of Henry Vaughan*, ed. L. C. Martin. Oxford, 1957 [orig. 1914].
Witsius, Hermann. *De Oeconomia Foederum Dei Cum Hominbus*. Leeuwarden, 1677.
Yates, Frances. *The Art of Memory*. London, 1966.
_____. *Giordano Bruno and the Hermetic Tradition*. Chicago, 1964.
_____. *Theatre of the World*. London, 1969.